The Coming of Age of Community

'Erik Bichard's new book is a hard-headed look at the lessons learned from a generation of community-led regeneration, rich with case studies as well as analysis, and will be useful for students as well as practitioners trying to come to grips with an era where we need to be bottom up as well as top down if we hope to address global challenges like climate change, resource scarcity and inequality.'

– Hank Dittmar, Special Adviser to HRH The
Prince of Wales for Global Urbanisation

People organising to protect their environment is not a new phenomenon, but the groups that have been pushing for environmental change since the 1970s have not convinced sufficient numbers to make sustainable decisions or to lead sustainable lives. Governments have serially failed to do the job at the international level. Now, climate change, resource depletion and widening social aspirations threaten to destabilise human society unless sustainable change can be influenced from another direction. *The Coming of Age of the Green Community* explores the activities of a new generation of community-led initiatives that may herald the beginnings of the next wave of activism. Erik Bichard combines the testimonies of dozens of group activists with historic evidence and the views of a range of commentators from a variety of disciplines to put forward reasons why some green community groups succeed while others fail. He concludes with a valuable prescription for both existing and emerging groups on how to be sustainable, both over time and in their actions. This book addresses one of the key questions of the twenty-first century: has the local perspective on this universal concern finally come of age?

Erik Bichard is Professor of Regeneration and Sustainable Development at the University of Salford, UK.

Routledge Explorations in Environmental Studies

The Coming of Age of the Green Community

My neighbourhood, my planet

Erik Bichard

Routledge
Taylor & Francis Group

LONDON AND NEW YORK

First published 2014
by Routledge
2 Park Square, Milton Park, Abingdon, Oxfordshire OX14 4RN

and by Routledge
711 Third Avenue, New York, NY 10017

First issued in paperback 2014

Routledge is an imprint of the Taylor and Francis Group, an informa business

British Library Cataloguing in Publication Data
A catalogue record for this book is available from the British Library

Library of Congress Cataloging in Publication Data
Bichard, Erik.
The coming of age of the green community : my neighbourhood, my planet / Erik Bichard.
pages cm. -- (Routledge explorations in environmental studies)
Includes bibliographical references and index.
1. Environmentalism. 2. Green movement. 3. Community organization.
4. Political participation. 5. Sustainable living. I. Title.
GE195.B54 2013
304.2--dc23
2013011092

ISBN 978-0-415-51761-4 (hbk)
ISBN 978-1-138-91515-2 (pbk)
ISBN 978-0-203-10947-2 (ebk)

Typeset in Times New Roman
by Taylor & Francis Books

For Dr Sheila Bichard – then and now

Contents

Acknowledgements

Most of the credit for this book goes to the community members and activists (both named and unnamed) who spent long hours with me explaining their initiatives and the aspects that characterised their communities. But they were also asked about their personal motivations, influences and life paths and invariably shared all of this with generosity and hospitality. I am very grateful to everyone who was prepared to give up time they could have spent making their communities even better to speak to me.

I would also like to thank Professor Ludger Basten for helping me to get connected in Freiburg. Danesch Missaghian for his field translation skills and good company on the road. Carlos Kearns for his support and guidance around the 'Burgh'. Finally, I am really grateful to Professor Steve Curwell and Julie Collins, who were prepared to listen to me think out loud with good grace, patience and valuable advice.

1 Is green activism turning a new page?

The environmental movement X.0

On 21 June 2011, Charles Secrett, a former leader of Friends of the Earth, wrote an open letter to the Green Movement (Secrett, 2011). The letter asked activists to reconsider the way they sought to change societal opinion about the environment and the adoption of sustainable practices. In his challenge, he asked the Movement to accept that 'tried and tested campaign tactics, based on protest and outrage at the incompetence of governments and industry, are not working'. He wanted them to 'break free from a perpetually defensive mode, and go on the offensive'.

He continued by accepting that there was a lack of political will to make the changes that were needed and called for non-government organisations (NGOs) to co-ordinate their efforts to more powerful effect under one banner: 'For people, for the planet'. Under a joint manifesto, the NGOs could gain consensus for this from both the public and sympathetic politicians. He warned that simple interaction was not the same as real power which 'resides with voters, tax-payers and constituents. No government can rule without citizen consent.' He suggested recruiting allies among 'scientists, gardeners, fishers, farmers, foresters, sports-people, outdoor recreationalists and tens of millions of people who depend on a clean, healthy environment'. His rallying cry was for the groups to organise locally in every constituency to build formidable alliances between their own supporters, other community groups, unions and local businesses.

His call was effectively to re-boot all campaigns and 'spark the reasonable revolution'. This is an interesting choice of words as it could be argued that a reliance on reason (the orderly consideration of the facts leading to a rational decision) had served the environmental movement badly over the years. There has been a deluge of facts transmitted by the media, governments and non-government bodies warning about the damage humans have been doing to their environment. These warnings have covered shrinking habitats like the rainforests to the coral reefs. They have chronicled the advance of the deserts, the acidification of the forests and the seas, the erosion of the ozone layer, and the accelerating extinction rates of flora and fauna. The past decade has been dominated by the effects of global warming, including melting ice caps and glaciers, stronger and more frequent storms, and devastating droughts and floods. These reports have been regularly punctuated with stories of ecological tragedies caused by oil spills, nuclear accidents and industrial contamination of the ground, air and water.

The difficulty for the environmental movement has been that their own reaction to these assaults on global ecosystems has not been the same as that of the rest of the population. It is easy to devise a campaign if the designer shares the same values as the audience, but more of a challenge if the majority need another kind of motivation to pay attention to the message. The environmental movement has often treated the wider public's ambivalence to environmental degradation as a malfunction in civic society that could be corrected if only people were made to understand that there is a crisis in their midst. The increase in charitable giving when images of people in distress are shown on television is encouragement that this tactic works. Successful public information campaigns also offered precedents for success. The images of carnage as a result of road traffic accidents and tombstones (promoting the use of seat belts in cars and the practice of safe sex in reaction to the threat of AIDS, respectively) were effective in their time at changing public behaviour. In these cases, the reluctance to give up personal preferences was weaker than the belief that to ignore the advice would mean danger of death to the viewer and to those close to them.

The problem for those hoping to use the same tactics to reduce the use of fossil fuels and resource consumption through energy conservation or by shopping less, for example, is that the behavioural context for these decisions differs from the AIDS and seatbelt campaigns. With a threat like climate change, there is no clear cause and effect connection associated with behaviour change, either for the individual or the implications of the individual's action on others. The consequences of a failure to act are not strong enough to conquer the personal preferences that allow the individual to discount or ignore the message to change.

This may lead to the conclusion that all forms of information to influence pro-environmental behaviour are doomed to fail. However, while it is probably the case that the majority of people will not act on information alone, there may be a place for well-aimed messages within a more integrated approach. Those planning behaviour change campaigns need to appreciate that human reaction to environmental conditions is complex. People often need to overcome the urge to wait for more conclusive evidence before they act. This uncertainty is often fed by a mistaken need by the media to present a balanced argument, regardless of the consensus supporting one side or the other. People are also tempted to downplay the likelihood that their lives will be significantly affected by environmental impacts. If the threat were really serious, they would expect the state to step in to protect its citizens. The time and effort necessary to re-assess one's lifestyle and make changes to common habits and patterns are certainly not beyond anyone's capabilities, but it is often far easier to resist the temptation to give in to fatalism or feelings of futility (Lorenzoni *et al.*, 2007) or to devote energy to reversing seemingly insuperable odds. Most people are happy to carry on regardless of the dire warnings

Thinking about these aspects of human perception led me to write *Positively Responsible*, with the organisational psychologist, Cary Cooper (Bichard and Cooper, 2008). Up until that point I had been advising business and government officials on how to be more sustainable. I wanted to try to understand the extent to which aspects of human behaviour other than cognitive processes could explain why people take unsustainable decisions. My thinking at the time was that if all aspects of behaviour could be addressed, then policy-makers would have a far better chance of developing strategies that made more people, willingly, live and work in a sustainable manner.

Pacing change in an increasingly unsustainable world

After *Positively Responsible*, I focused my academic career and research on ways to engage the public (and elected officials) using a range of different behavioural approaches. Some of this work was for the Environment Agency of England and Wales (Bichard and Kazmierczak, 2009). The study initially dealt with the attitudes of householders towards buying energy conservation and flood protection measures for their homes. The report concluded that:

> Fact-based campaigns aimed at changing people's behaviour by influencing rational cognitive processes were not effective because behaviour does not change as a result of knowing more, and because there is no clear cause and effect connection between climate change and the actions required to address it.

The report went on to say:

> While social norms (what other people do or are perceived to approve of) have a significant impact on the behaviour of individuals, this is dependent on an acute consciousness that the tide is turning and that new behaviour has become commonplace.

Unless these conditions can be met, it puts Secrett's revolution based on reason at serious risk of failing, and so it has proved to date.

And yet this does not undermine Secrett's main contention that tactics have to change if more people are to adopt the means to a sustainable life. Often when messages are delivered to a target audience using a passive media like television, radio or print, they involve a generic plea to residents to take action or to do their part. But people are more likely to take action for other reasons such as reacting to the behaviour of the trusted people around them, being attracted by incentives or financial motives, or learning from a previous experience. Simply knowing what to do often is not a strong enough reason to take action. Although education campaigns can positively influence knowledge or attitudes, they are largely ineffective at creating lasting changes in behaviour (Schultz and Tabanico, 2008).

This is why Secrett's advice to 'organise in every constituency' may be the best way forward for national and international environmental pressure groups. Ajzen and Fishbein (1980) showed that there is a relationship between attitudes and behaviour that combines facts (do I understand the problem?; and do I know what to do about it?) with the emotional (do I care about the problem?; if I act, will it work?; and what will people around me think of my actions?). This complex mix of emotions, thoughts and the predisposition to do something makes simple education and awareness campaigns to use the car less, for example, or stop flying to holiday destinations almost a non-starter. However, those who are working within their communities, talking and interacting with both the willing and the reluctant on sustainability issues are, on this evidence, more likely to build an effective movement.

This call to the community is reinforced by the perception that the world's environmental and social justice problems are unlikely to be solved by governments. This statement might have been met with disbelief and even shock just a generation ago. But the lack of international consensus on international climate change in Kyoto in 1997 set the scene for a series of similar disappointments that left activists with the distinct feeling that they are on their own. This despair at a failure to reach consensus at an international level has led to the conclusion by some outside the movement that environmentalism, or certainly the ability of environmentalists to influence global decisions, has reached the end of the line.

In their provocative essay, 'The Death of Environmentalism', Shellenberger and Nordhaus (2004) argue that modern environmentalism has outlived its original usefulness and that it should now make way for another movement that could continue to fight for Nature without the baggage that has become associated with the environmental agenda. The authors did not suggest what should replace the old regime. At an event to discuss the essay at Harvard, Ted Nordhaus explained:

> When you look at the environmental movement, at the great ecological challenges that the planet is faced with, that humanity is faced with, environmentalism has proven utterly incapable of addressing them. The reason we called for environmentalism's death is so that we could call for a new movement that can address these challenges.
>
> (*Harvard University Gazette*, May 2005)

A few years earlier, Michael Jacobs (1999) had caused consternation in Britain with his Fabian pamphlet, *Environmental Modernisation: The New Labour Agenda,* in which he made a similar claim. He said that environmentalism was too important to be left to the environmental movement because governments had stopped listening to them. Jacob's tack was to appropriate the notion of 'modernisation' (popular with the New Labour government at the time) to re-frame environmental issues in a way that would catch the eye of aspiring ministers. The tactic backfired with established British environmentalists like Jonathon Porritt angrily responding that it was radical green groups that made it possible for him and others to operate closer to the British establishment. This was partly because compared to radical Greens he represented the acceptable face of the environmental lobby, but more because they were skilled in raising issues in a stark, sometimes sensationalist manner that caught the media's (and hence the public's) eyes and ears and put pressure on elected representatives and businesses.

The journey

Modern environmental activism is sometimes traced back to the first of Gaylord Nelson's Earth Days on 22 April 1970. This was one of the first attempts to publicly communicate the fragility of Nature and the finite extent of the Earth's resources. Of course, there were many notable examples of individual and group efforts that had preceded this. John Muir founded the Sierra Club and convinced President Roosevelt to create the first National Park in the Yosemite Valley in the 1890s. Marjory Stoneham Douglas staunchly supported the protection of the Everglades from the 1920s. In England, John Ruskin's influential writings in Victorian times (he lived between 1819 and1900), highlighted the destructive influence of the Industrial Revolution on Nature and he is credited with inspiring the modern British environmental movement. One of his earliest followers was Octavia Hill, who is not only credited with some of the earliest attempts to build social housing, but co-founded the National Trust in 1895. The Trust is still the largest membership group in the UK and is devoted to preserving national built heritage and open spaces. Just over 30 years later, Patrick Abercrombie, the architect and urban designer, founded the Campaign for the Protection of Rural England (previously the Council for the Preservation of Rural England) to ensure urban sprawl did not engulf the countryside.

The more radical strands of environmental protest such as Greenpeace and Friends of the Earth did not reach Britain until the 1970s, but in membership terms were still dwarfed by the more genteel, countryside-orientated organisations. For a time, these radical forces were very successful in bringing environmental issues to the fore. Campaigns were often most effective when one individual issue that had general appeal was singled out. Endangered animals (the blue whale, the giant panda and the Bengal tiger, for example) helped to introduce the public to campaigns on the wider issue of habitat loss, including the rainforests and the coral reefs. Campaigns on the exploitation of renewable resources, including fisheries (by highlighting the plight of species like the tuna and the swordfish) and logging in wilderness forests were also very effective. But while these campaigns have to varying degrees influenced individual policies and laws, they do not represent a collective popular shift in favour of the environment. It is this failure to galvanise society that leaves the environmental movement open to the criticism that it has failed to make its mark on human behaviour.

Many commentators talk about the need to foster a new world-view where inequality is banished and lives are not judged by conspicuous consumption. Paul Hawken (2007: 22) sums this up when he talks about how humans view progress. The dilemma, he says, lies between 'single measures of material accumulation such as GDP ... and the health of the earth and its inhabitants'. While the environmental movement has been reasonably successful in raising issues that stem from a failure to protect 'the health of the earth', it has been less successful in influencing a sizeable proportion of its constituency to maintain and enhance that health through the adoption of sustainable business practices and lifestyles.

This stagnation of influence prompts attention to be redirected away from centrally organised groups, to the heart of the communities where these impacts will be felt by every individual. There have always been people who have enjoyed coming together to improve their village or neighbourhood. A good number of these would probably be unconcerned about anything other than their immediate surroundings. They would be unlikely to describe themselves as environmentalists, but would undoubtedly be passionate about their environment. Their world-view could easily support the status quo without making any kind of link between their use of cars or aircraft and the increasing frequency of droughts or floods affecting their gardens.

A typical example of this local championing of the environment is the Britain in Bloom movement. Started by the British Tourist Board in 1963, the competition was inspired by the French Fleurissement de France competition. It invited towns and villages to improve the appearance of their communities by working together to plant hanging baskets and lavish floral borders in competition with others to win national recognition. The management of Britain in Bloom was taken over by the Royal Horticultural Society (RHS) in 2002 and the competing villages, towns and city neighbourhoods are now judged on a wider set of measures, including their horticultural excellence, their environmental responsibility and their community participation.

The RHS was intent on bringing a rather quaint annual event into the twenty-first century when it took it over. In 2011, it published a report that sought to understand the far-reaching impacts of 'Britain's biggest community horticultural movement' (RHS, 2011). The report looked at the three potential areas of influence for a sustainable community initiative, including the social, economic and environmental implications of participation. The report concluded that participating communities benefited from enhanced environments. But they also gained from stronger ties between people, a reduction in anti-social behaviour, increased skills and confidence, and health and well-being. The emphasis seemed to be (perhaps surprisingly) not on the environmental or economic imperatives, but on the social sphere of the three-legged stool of sustainability. People said that they enjoyed getting to know neighbours who had formerly been just nodding acquaintances, sometimes for many years. For many residents, it was the act of collective action that seemed to be the most pleasing aspect of the competition. This is a recurring theme from many community engagement studies and may go some way to explaining why campaigns that focus on more strategic matters which require individual action (petitions, sending donations or writing to elected representatives, for example) have not made as many inroads into society as the environmental movement might have hoped.

While national initiatives like Britain in Bloom can galvanise pro-environmental action for positive reasons, many other communities come together to protect the place where they live in common opposition to a perceived or actual threat. In the north-west of England where I have lived for 30 years, there have been high-profile campaigns by local communities against silica sand and aggregate mines, clinical waste incinerators, waste-to-energy plants (including a biomass-fuelled power station), wind turbine farms (both onshore and offshore), numerous large housing schemes (including an eco-town concept) and the exploration of shale gas. While all of these developments were opposed by people who argued that they should not be built anywhere, some would be supported by the objectors if only a more suitable site could be identified. It is simplistic to label all such objectors NIMBYs (Not In My Back Yard) but often the reasons for objecting are complicated and personal. Devine-Wright (2012) interviewed over 500 objectors in the south-east of England and found that the factors that made people oppose new development included their age, whether there were children in the family, the length of time they had lived in the community, both the positive and negative impacts of the development, trust in the developer, and procedural justice.

It is perhaps obvious, particularly with a natural aversion to change, limited information and built-in suspicion of authority that people will tend towards a position of opposition to new and intrusive development in their area. The more interesting question is whether people associate their actions with pro-environmental behaviour or whether they assemble reasons, including concern for the environment, to back up their gut rejection of the proposal. Collective action in the face of a clear and present threat (like the construction of a new clinical waste incinerator) will understandably generate strong emotions. But if the community can see off the threat (either by influencing elected officials to throw out the application or to present arguments at a public inquiry), then the need to collaborate goes away. While some revert to previous lifestyles, others are indelibly affected by the arguments they used in their fight and it can change the way they think about the wider world.

Occasionally, the act of assembling and co-operating generates a community spirit that is hard to give up, even after victory has been assured. This is the effect that some participants described in the Britain in Bloom survey. It is common to hear the participants in other pro-environment movements voice the same opinions (see the British Gas Green Streets initiative (Platt, 2011) and the RELISH initiative   (www.relish.org/downloads/RELISH_12_MONTH_REPORT.pdf) for examples of this). This does prompt the question about whether the thirst for community participation opportunities may allow policy-makers to circumvent some of the arguments for why people need to adopt pro-environmental stances. As we will see, the transformative effective of community action did have a discernible effect on elements of a whole region in Germany, leading to action on a range of issues that were not part of the original reason for organising. In England, there have been very successful community groups that have actively avoided tackling the issue of sustainable living head-on. Their tactic has been to attract participation through the common denominator of food. Once social interaction is established and trust advanced between community members, more profound conversations about the future of resource availability and threats like climate change become easier to initiate and more natural in their evolution.

The motivating forces that drive those who are willing to join global campaigns and those who are focused on protecting or enhancing their local environment are not mutually exclusive. It is perfectly feasible for people to occupy both spaces, provided they have the time to devote to multiple initiatives. There are many examples of this in the accounts that follow in this book. However, many of those who are featured here expressed a frustration that the global campaigns they supported were too impersonal and did not engage them as activists beyond signing petitions or donating money. These people needed to be regularly and actively engaged in pro-environmental activity. They needed to be able to see that their opinions were being heard even though they might not see much evidence that they were being heeded.

It also was evident when listening to modern environmental activists that they do not fit the caricatures that used to be levelled at the environmental movement. Disparaging phrases like 'sandal-wearing muesli knitters' were uttered by those who disapproved of those they perceived to be living alternative lifestyles outside the norms of society. People who spoke up for the movement were painted as strident, Left-leaning and opinionated. They were described as mistrustful of the establishment and large corporations in particular. They were expected to be very critical of people who conspicuously and wastefully consumed for pleasure or for status without a thought for the global poor or the environment.

It is unlikely that any environmental activist would recognise themselves in all these terms, but would probably admit to elements of this description. What is interesting is that those interviewed for this book do not conform to many of these common identifiers or stereotypes of the environmental movement. Instead they are just as likely to come from conservative or religious backgrounds and will have been working within the establishment right up until and beyond the point when they felt they needed to take action. A substantial minority come from the caring professions and have transferred skills learned in healthcare, social work and community support to bring about sustainable change. While there have been calls for the environmental movement to transform itself to meet a new twenty-first-century value set, evidence from these interviews suggests that this transformation could already be taking place.

Another change that is apparent from talking to activists now is that there has been a shift over the past ten years in the perception of the environmental threat to communities. This is particularly true when communities organise in reaction to climate change. Whereas previously co-operation occurred in the face of a local threat (such as a new mine or housing project), now pro-environmental activities are taking place in relation to a more generalised threat that has the potential to change local conditions in the future, but is not yet in evidence.

This revives memories of the old Friends of the Earth strap line 'think global, act local', which dates from the early 1970s. Now, with the rise of groups inspired by permaculture (Transition Towns), energy saving (Green Communities Network) and grow–cook–eat initiatives, local environmental activism may be finally making this link in greater numbers and to greater effect.

While time will tell if these changes become permanent, campaigners with longer memories will be asking if this is just another ebb and flow along the timeline of the movement's chequered history. The effects of interruptions to oil supplies and economic downturns since the 1970s have often put paid to a burgeoning pro-environment momentum. Elkington (1999) explains that the second OPEC oil shock (1978–9) and the election of Ronald Reagan to the US presidency in 1981 combined to encourage rapid economic growth and suppress regulation which undermined efforts to control environmental impacts.

The discovery of the hole in the ozone layer in 1985 and the *Exxon Valdez* oil tanker disaster in Alaska in 1989 helped to put the environment and environmentalists back in the public eye. At this time the membership of campaigning green groups was rapidly increasing. For Friends of the Earth in the UK, the numbers rose from 15,000 in 1970 to 190,000 in 1990. A similar rise from 30,000 in 1979 to 400,000 in 1990 was achieved by Greenpeace (Marquand, 2008). But even as the world was meeting in 1992 in Brazil for the first Earth Summit, economic recession was again sidelining the environmentalists' call to invest in pro-environmental improvements in favour of any kind of job creation.

Since Elkington summarised these first 'waves' and 'downwaves' of environmental action, there has been a slow but steady narrative about the next overriding threat: climate change. While there continues to be a rear-guard action of a small group (dubbed climate deniers), the overwhelming evidence from the scientific community is beginning to have an effect on the public psyche. This concern can increase in the wake of severe weather events such as hurricanes Katrina in 2005 and Sandy in 2012 and the heat wave that caused thousands of fatalities in Europe in 2003.

In the aftermath of the economic crisis of 2008–9 there was real hope among environmental economists that a corner might have been turned. This surge of optimism came from a belief that the collapse finally put to rest the mantra of the free market advocates that the system would always right itself. Their opponents argued that the collapse showed that the current regime was no longer fit for purpose. An early convert was the UN General Secretary, Ban Ki-moon, who started to make speeches about the need for a 'Green New Deal' (UN News Centre, 2008). President Barack Obama announced plans for a new 'green fiscal stimulus package', which included a doubling of renewable energy in three years, and a comprehensive programme of energy conservation retrofits for public buildings and two million homes (Goldenberg, 2009).Tim Jackson's *Prosperity Without Growth?* set out a strategy for a sustainable economy and pointed out the consequences of failing to grasp the opportunity for change (Jackson, 2009).

But just a few years later many were concerned that the momentum had run out of steam. After presenting his model for a new green economy to leaders at the Rio +20 conference in 2012, Jackson found that the scare had not been frightening enough to make government leaders turn away from the old patterns of consumption and production. He said on his return, 'Disappointment doesn't quite cover it. It's a staggering failure of responsibility' (Confino, 2012). Others were worried that this loss of momentum had started to trickle down to the local level. Chris Church, a green community organiser said: 'The challenge for any community group or activist is increasingly "What can we do that will really make a difference?" … The optimism and energy that characterised local action in 2008–10 [is] harder to find.' He went on to observe that public concern about the environment seems to come and go. He says that: 'Opinion polls show that most people accept and are concerned about climate change, but they are not engaged or active. There are millions of such people – far more than the active deniers and sceptics' (Church, 2012).

Recently, different disciplines have become interested in answering questions on a willingness to act on climate change. In a collection of essays edited by Sally Weintrobe (2013), psychotherapists and other professionals write about their understanding of the reaction to climate change, and the tendency to inaction in particular. The book describes a number of ways people deal with the bad news associated with the consequences of global warming. Some can't accept the facts because they think they are too fanciful to be true, while others suspect that there is an ulterior motive for those who are delivering the message, making them doubt whether they are telling the truth. Some of the most interesting observations come in an essay by Lertzman (2013) on the 'Myth of Apathy'. The proposition here is that people fail to act to reduce the impact of climate change not because they don't care, but because they care too much. Her conclusion is that the thought that the life-supporting elements of the Earth are being undermined is so disturbing that it makes people park the issue in a part of their mind where it will not inhibit their ability to function on a day-to-day basis.

Psychotherapists say that this is dangerous for our mental health, but it could also explain the growth in green activism. Framed in the right way by the right people, taking action in response to these disturbing facts could be embraced enthusiastically by those who have been seeking a way to respond. It may be a relief to accept impending catastrophe if the anxiety can be channelled into activity that is working towards a solution. Even if this effort eventually proves to be ineffective, the act of participation with others is a much healthier choice than waiting powerlessly for the community's demise.

Alone, together

When looking at whether green community action has now come of age, it is relevant to ask not only whether the latest wave of interest is going to leave a longer legacy than its predecessors, but in view of the time bomb of climate change, whether it will make the break-through changes that are required. If it is, what will be needed to overcome the usual diversions and obstacles and make this wave permanent? One way of answering this question is to turn to the philosopher Mary Midgley, who contends that selfishness, as a survival tactic, is inefficient, and that eventually co-operation has to intervene to avert disaster (Midgley, 2005). She thinks that we are programmed to take self-interested action at all times, particularly in time of plenty, because 'When things are going well, we simply don't believe in disasters. Long-term prudence, reaching beyond the accepted routine precautions of everyday life is therefore an extraordinary feeble motive.' But Midgley says this will change to an alternative strategy as we approach 'the increasing probability of environmental disaster'. No amount of 'individualist propaganda can destroy the corporate element in morals'. She says:

> Even when there is no conscious talk of duty, the people who work in any co-operative enterprise – school, firm, shop, orchestra, theatrical company, teenage gang, political party, football team [or local environmental group] – find it thoroughly natural to act as if they had a duty to [that community] if it is in some way threatened.

She hopes that:

> we could accept the overwhelming existing evidence of a 'terrestrial emergency' without needing to be hit by a direct disaster. But whatever causes that belief to be accepted, once it becomes so, there is surely little doubt about the duty it lies upon us.

There may well be evidence in new and emerging local environment groupings that supports Midgley's elegant explanation of the motivation for collective pro-environmental action. There are many people who, for a range of reasons, feel the impending threat to the ecological balance of global systems and opt to do what they can to avert disaster. However, others are likely to be motivated for all kinds of different reasons such as a deep sense of place and the fear of losing this, the pleasure that comes with working with others for a common goal or simply because they respect the people who asked them to get involved.

Before we run away with the optimistic thought that humanity will rally in the face of the impending threats to society, we need to apply some form of reality check. Will the environmental and social justice movements prevail over exploitation of the human and the natural world? There have been some significant turning points and victories overcoming seemingly insurmountable odds in the past. The abolition of slavery, votes for women, rights to education, and access to health care and shelter have spread throughout the world although there is still a long way to go before any of these are universal. Global action on protecting the ozone layer through the Montreal Protocol was achieved and tight control over the exploitation of resources in the Arctic and Antarctic regions are strained but being maintained. A recent initiative to protect ocean resources in international waters may signal the beginnings of greater protection for oceanic ecosystems (Doyle, 2013).

There have also been local successes for the environmental movement. Greenpeace did manage to stop the Brent Spar platform from being scrapped at sea. There have been bans on shale gas exploitation in some areas and a few entire countries. The control of illegal logging has improved in some though not all regions. But many of the underlying problems still persist and the accounts in this book show that green community activists are not hopeful that these problems will ever be overcome. Given this depressing analysis, it is remarkable that, far from giving up, communities are re-doubling their efforts to make sure that their people are protected from the worst excesses of the impending impacts. They do not trust authorities to solve these problems and seek to fill this gap themselves, often rejecting outside organisations who have offered to help them organise locally.

This self-sufficiency of purpose translates into a realisation that individuals cannot afford to try to solve or even ride out environmental problems by themselves, holed up in their own homes. Another feature of the accounts in this book is the effort that is going on to engage with people of different backgrounds and motivations. This energetic, patient, incisive work is seen as essential to the success of each initiative. For some time it was obvious to me that community groups had to play a key role in building an 'I-will-if-you-will' culture. This is something that social psychologists call 'norm-based' behaviour (see Halpern and Bates, 2004; Cialdini 2004, 2007). This was reinforced by reading the work of authors like Ginsborg (2005) and Hawken (2007).

Ginsborg's interest in the ability of civil society to further the potential for democracy considers that community groups can be an agent for action in a variety of ways. They can 'give some collective form to an individual's sense of indignation or anger, or simple desire to do something now'. However, to be successful, Ginsborg thinks that community groups 'need to be places where individuals feel welcome and be able to express their opinions freely ...

and ... sceptical of all hierarchies, including those in their own midst' (Ginsborg, 2005: 139).

Hawken looks at community groups from the more focused context of an environmentalist who is heartened and impressed at the way people come together in opposition to factors that cause global harm. His view is that the conditions that affect the world have fashioned a global movement that is played out in local contexts. While he believes that this is the biggest movement in the world, he acknowledges that 'concerned individuals have to work out [how to respond] for themselves and find colleagues to mentor them'. Hawken believes that movements are 'the expression of changed attitudes, and how each person comes to realise his responsibility to a greater whole is a unique experience' (Hawken, 2007: 23).

The reality is that there are some communities that have organised well to vent their opposition to a threat, who co-operate to improve their local environment or lessen their impact on their surroundings. The following chapters will tell a number of their stories and will explain how they came to be so effective in their own ways. But there are many other communities that have either failed to make an effective difference or have not been able to mount a collective effort at all. Ginsborg (2005: 140) explains that 'the truth is that civil society is often a mess'. He points out that, with a wide range of personalities, agendas and habits, it is 'no easy task to absorb and amalgamate all this to find an acceptable democratic forum'. And yet many communities are continuing to do this in support of the environment with increased frequency and passion, and in the absence of an external organising force.

There is ample evidence from many other sources that reinforces this view. Community groups can make a difference to the way neighbourhoods react to threats and can galvanise resilience. They can have a vital role as the translating link between government sources and individual residents, and can interpret the growing threats from climate change and resource depletion for those who are concerned but have not fully understood what is around the corner or how they can respond to avoid its worst effects.

The British environmental think tank Green Alliance goes further and considers that it is 'not possible to crack climate change without reinvigorating civic responsibility. We'll never be able to make our lifestyles more sustainable without the social cohesion that makes it feel good to be doing these things as part of something bigger' (Scott, 2010). There are several reasons for this assertion. The first and arguably the most powerful is that the people who make up community groups are the most likely trusted messengers/persuaders on the doorstep or at community gatherings.

That people listen more to those they know and trust was shown in the context of energy conservation by the psychologist Wesley Schultz (Schultz *et al.* 2007). He found that while people would say that they were motivated to buy low-energy light bulbs to protect the environment, their actions were often only prompted by a visit to their neighbour's house. There they saw how that individual had committed to the purchase of a particular product, successfully installed it and said that it worked.

A further, less obvious benefit of community groups lies in their staying power. The Green Alliance report explains this by stating that 'The on-going interaction also means that behaviours are more likely to be sustained over the long term, as they benefit from collective support and positive reinforcement.' The introduction of energy-saving measures in a home will have an immediate and lasting effect on energy consumption, but the full potential of this will never be realised without an accompanying change in the mindset of those who use the building on a regular basis. Any community group, regardless of its core purpose (faith, arts, sports, single-issue campaign, etc.) has the potential to influence short-term behaviour and convert this into longer-term habitual behaviour. They do need the capacity and resources to deliver the message to the neighbourhood or stakeholder group. But if these are in place they might begin with influencing changes in purchasing behaviour, and then continue this work to help others to change lifestyles as long as the group gains support and is sustained in the community.

The original motivation to write this book was to explore current green community activism with a view to confirming the assumptions we made during the research with the Environment Agency. A limited trial in an urban residential area was set up to test whether behaviour change tactics could be effective to motivate people to act sustainably. The trial was a qualified success, with a number of residents responding to the strategy. A full account of the experiment is set out in Chapter 5. The main findings of the study were that a number of behaviour change tactics could be combined in one strategy to overcome some of the natural reticence to participate in pro-environment schemes. The report of the trial (Bichard and Thurairajah, 2011) concluded that a triple-track strategy should be applied to future schemes where pro-environment behaviour is required. This includes intervention with the right information at the optimum point in the decision-making process; the use of incentives that support the proposition; and surrounding the reluctant and the doubters with evidence that others accept the change and would approve of those who joined them. The last element was supplied by a green community group who acted as the agents and facilitators on behalf of the academics. It was their presence that gave residents the understanding that others were interested in energy conservation and flood protection. The group continued to work in the community after the study was finished and helped to create a permanent organisation of green activists among the residents.

The message for policy-makers from this work was that sustainable strategies could be more successful if green community groups were engaged in promoting them. This tactic would result in better value for money by investing in local networks rather than relying on more remote forms of motivation or outside agencies. The assumption is that some form of community group is already in place in almost every neighbourhood. The original investigations for this book were geared to determine whether this resource had been overlooked as a potent force to augment or catalyse sustainable change instigated mainly by local and central government.

What transpired as I moved between communities in England, Germany and the USA was something quite different. Green community groups may have been around for over a century, but it appeared as each interviewee gave their story that something was changing, both in terms of the reasons for environmental activism and the way that the groups were organised. Several factors were at work in this process of change. There were recurring themes of an affront to justice and a lack of faith in hierarchies. In particular, there was mistrust in the ability of government to achieve any of the goals that the communities had identified as being of paramount importance. Most were very clear about global conditions. They understood that life in their areas would be getting progressively more difficult if trends continued. But the magnitude of the task did not undermine their intention to try to make a difference where they lived.

Another recurring theme was the way the activists characterised themselves. They often resisted the adoption of a label of any kind and many, though not all, said that they would not consider themselves to be environmentalists. They made this statement in the full knowledge that they were devoting a significant amount of their time to pro-environmental activity. They told stories of commitment and hardship. They explained their numerous reasons and motivations that kept them pushing for better environmental conditions. I have tried to record their hopes and fears for the future, and their demands for support and political change which they feel they need but do not expect in order to achieve their goals.

The accounts in this book cover examples of communities organising in the USA, the UK and Germany. This is in no way to infer that these countries are more energetic, or are even leading the way in modern green community action. The examples were partly chosen for their proximity to my base in the north-west of England and partly by reputation. For example, while there is anti-fracking activity in many countries, the groups in Pennsylvania have been among the largest and most vociferous and have fought for a longer period of time than many others. Similarly, the focus on Vauban in Freiburg was to delve a little deeper into a community that has a reputation for being one of the most sustainable in Europe.

There are also many communities outside Europe and North America that are fighting to preserve vital resources against powerful vested interests. However, this book's focus is primarily on those communities in post-industrial places where people have started to anticipate the implications associated with diminishing access to cheap resources (food, energy, etc.). They are places where people have been used to state support and are now realising that the state may not be able to look after everyone in the face of changes due to, in particular, global warming. Often but not exclusively urban in origin, European and North American communities are, at this time responding the most to these influences. The contention here is that if environmental community action is going to be rejuvenated to help people cope with the new environmental, social and economic landscape of the early twenty-first century, the instigators need to have experienced a combination of the plentiful but wasteful lifestyles of richer economies and the pressures that come from the decline of those economies just at a time when investment in resilience is required.

If austerity economics stretches out from a few post-2008 years to a decade and beyond, the impact of climate change on jobs, infrastructure, energy and food (among other factors) may limit support for the most vulnerable in hitherto affluent societies. It is this confluence of unsustainable factors that may lead some communities to start to take matters into their own hands, and it is this type of organising principle that I was seeking out when I chose the communities to visit for the book.

2   Living with the gold standard

Origins of a legend

Sustainable community legend has it that sometime in the early 1990s an architect and a biologist sat down together in a suburb of a small town in south-west Germany and wondered if it was possible to create housing that would surpass all expectations for sustainable living. The houses would run entirely on renewable energy and the waste produced by the inhabitants. They would be built by their future occupants from locally produced materials. There would be no cars to interrupt the placid, healthy and safe streetscape and the community would be democratically collectively governed by its residents. It is difficult to confirm that this conversation ever happened, or, if it did, whether the two protagonists were themselves responsible for what happened next, but the project has certainly been realised. Almost 6,000 people now live on around 16 hectares of land that is now one of the biggest attractions on the eco-tourism circuit: Freiburg-Vauban.

The key date for Vauban was 1992. In this year the city was chosen as Germany's Environmental Capital. The city's own publication, *Green City Freiburg: Approaches to Sustainability* explains that the title was conferred for 'pioneering achievements such as the installation of an early warning system for smog and ozone pollution, pesticide bans, [its] returnable packaging measures, [and] for its traffic and transport policy' (Breyer *et al.*, 2011).

Later Freiburg-Vauban was presented as 'German Best Practice' at the UN Habitat II Conference 1996 in Istanbul, reinforcing its sustainable claims, and it won the 'Sustainable Capital' accolade in 2004. Today, the reputation of Freiburg as a 'Green City' has spread around the globe. In just 20 years a small university town with a population of around 230,000, known more for its wine growing than its solar settlement, has been transformed into a sustainable paradise.

But 1992 was also the year that French finally withdrew their occupying army (a remnant from the Second World War) from Freiburg, leaving a large barracks complex in a neglected district on the edge of town called Vauban. Vauban is now the jewel in Freiburg's green community crown. The question for those seeking to emulate this achievement is whether the claims stand up to scrutiny; should Vauban be the role model for the next generation of green activists? Has the Freiburg green transformation (with Vauban in the vanguard) been the result of a collective realisation that sustainability should be at the heart of all development, or did a few far-sighted officials and politicians realise that the agenda could be a way of fast-forwarding the city's sleepy economic progress on the wave of pro-environmental feeling?

Certainly Vauban deserves its green reputation, based on low-carbon energy achievements alone. Over 40 self-build design collectives were formed; many by idealistic groups who wanted to build the most sustainable housing they could afford. A number of housing co-operatives with similar goals sought to provide residential developments for low-income groups. There have been more than 100 Passiv-house standard units built to date which require no boiler or heating appliance because of their excellent insulation, air tightness and heat recovery properties. Of those, 30 were in the first two four-storey Passiv-houses ever built in Germany. Vauban also hosted some of the first net energy-producing houses or 'plus-energy houses' and has a wood-fuelled district heating system as well as enough solar electric arrays to make it one of the highest per-capita solar generators in any residential area.

The exclusion of cars in many parts of the district has given it a slightly misunderstood reputation as a traffic-free zone. The intended policy was to limit parking to the periphery of the residential area to reward those who did not own a vehicle. A car-pooling system was set up to ensure people had the means to travel when necessary and it was never the case that residents had to give up their cars to live in Vauban. However, the policy did create a child-friendly haven that attracted young couples and the average age of residents to this day is significantly lower than the national average. Cycle paths and cyclists are everywhere, and it is common to see cyclists with children in trailers in tow. When, in 2006, the tramline finally arrived in the district, it became even easier to avoid car ownership.

But what is Vauban really like?

Almut is a singer and teacher who runs a business from the community enterprise (DIVA) centre in the middle of Vauban. She came to Freiburg to study music in 1979 and found that she liked the city's atmosphere. She was from Munich where generally there was very little cultural mixing and society was dominated by a conservative outlook. Almut grew up in a more liberal household. When she came to Freiburg, she found it was a more tolerant and freer culture than Munich and she decided to stay. At first, she lived in a small apartment in the centre of town. But over a decade later when she began to have a family, she started looking for a bigger place to live, and one which was a little more child-friendly.

She said that in Germany (even in Freiburg), there were many rules governing noise and where children could and could not play. She heard about the Vauban project through newspapers and announcements on the radio and was attracted to the Baugruppen group idea that any group of people could band together to build their own block of flats or terraced house. She also liked the way traffic would be controlled, particularly as she did not own a car. But it was the idea of living an ecological lifestyle that really caught her imagination.

Almut does not consider herself to be particularly political, having been influenced by her father's ideas; he was a journalist and very knowledgeable and pragmatic about politicians' motives. But she had taken a keen interest in the acid rain debate, having lived in a forested area all her life and found it was dominating political discussion when she arrived in the city. However, it was the anti-nuclear debate that had raged around the site of Whyl nuclear power station (about 20 kilometres north-east of the city on the French border) that really engaged Almut's interest. Given planning permission a few years earlier in 1975, she was impressed to see the coalition that had come together to oppose the new power station included both the townsfolk of Freiburg and the farmers in the surrounding rural area. The farmers were not so much against nuclear power *per se*, but they were worried that the steam clouds would block out the sun on their fields. Regardless of the scientific grounds for their objection, the link between the rural and intellectual swayed the 'no-change' conservative politicians. This cross-regional alliance broke the acquiescent social norms and the key moment came when thousands of protesters mounted a mass trespass and occupied a muddy field, stopping the site preparation work. The government relented and the station was never built.

With the successful fight against the Whyl power station concluded, the region might have subsided into a quieter existence but for a campaign to close down another nearby nuclear reactor at Fessenheim. This would prove to be a harder job as the station is about 20 kilometres south-east of the city, but lies on the French side of the border. The campaign to close the site goes on to this day, and it is common to see the classic smiling sun 'Nein Danke' poster displayed in many windows throughout the city. The presence of the power station kept the issue boiling in the city, and it was partly this and partly the shock of the explosion at the Chernobyl nuclear plant in the Ukraine that led (in 1986) to Freiburg being one of the first German cities to fix a greenhouse gas target (a 25 per cent reduction by 2010) and to adopt a strategy to power the city through locally generated renewable energy. The programme included plans to reduce the consumption of energy, water and resources.

Many in the city say that the pro-environmental stance of Freiburg and the surrounding area became established after the battle of Whyl. Green Party politics became an attractive electoral choice in the region (Baden Wurttemberg) after this, culminating in the election of a Green Party mayor in 2002. In March 2011, a Green Party candidate became the regional prime minister for the first time.

Almut was successful in renting an apartment in the new eco-suburb of Vauban. In the early days there was no infrastructure so there had to be a make-do-and-mend spirit with neighbours helping each other out, generating a great communal spirit. Everyone was surrounded by new construction and there was constant talk on the streets and in the shops about the latest tiff with the city council or what had been proposed in the Forum meeting. Food co-operatives were being formed and common and semi-public areas debated and designed. She pointed out not everyone was hoping for a different way of living. These involved were a very mixed group both in terms of income and skills. There were academics and freelance young professionals, together with people with young families, students and public service workers.

It was a new experience for Almut to do things differently and together. She explains that it is the German way to report problems to the authorities without confronting the offender. In Vauban, they tried another way. In 2005, it was news when a family was evicted from a house they rented because the neighbours complained of too much noise. But these were isolated incidents and Almut maintains that when a problem was brewing, everyone agreed to meet and vent their frustrations, listen to each other and find the most acceptable solution. Where arbitration was required, the meeting invited the independent neighbourhood conflict resolution group KoKo (*Konstruktive Konfliktbearbeitung*) to attend. The group's services are free to community groups and rely on donations to train representatives in conflict resolution techniques. By invitation, they attended meetings where an argument had not been able to be settled informally and the KoKo representative would facilitate a discussion that would hopefully end in a compromise agreement. This did not work in all cases, but it was a welcome alternative to the standard German approach.

This rejection of governance by letter was very un-German and people generally welcomed open communication and the roundtable process. Almut feels that the spirit of co-operation does still exist in Vauban and hopes that this will not change in the future. She has also become an enthusiastic supporter of the district, volunteering to talk to the press and visiting academics. She often appears in newspapers and on-line articles, smiling for the cameras and explaining how good it is to live in a community that segregates cars from people and is mutually supportive and sustainable.

Because Vauban attracted a lot of people with children, Almut met a lot of people of her own age and outlook. This helped her to assimilate quickly into the community. This common demographic survives today and the atmosphere is dominated by children and their needs. Some things have changed though. From just a few hundred people in 1999, there are now thousands. The children who moved in at the start have now grown up to be teenagers and have different needs. Many like to escape what they see as the confines of Vauban for the more interesting entertainment in the city centre. There is an attempt to adapt existing spaces to maintain their interest but there are not many unused plots of land left in the area. Almut thinks that the challenge remains to offer these young adults reasons to stay in the district. The continuing influx of younger children is also proving to be a challenge necessitating an unprecedented third kindergarten and an enlarged primary school.

Almut says that she did not really arrive with an ideological vision of what Vauban was or should be. But over the years she does not feel that she has been disappointed. She is aware that others are not as happy as she has been with the development of the project. As she has got older, she accepts that things have stagnated from the dynamic atmosphere of the early days. Many of the moreidealistic people in her own housing development have left and been replaced by others who do not have the history or the appreciation of the original project. Her son is now a teenager and plays football on some of the green spaces near the marketplace. She knows that this is not really allowed, but everyone accepts that it needs to be tolerated or the place would deteriorate into the kind of rule-bound, childless places many had fled in the first place.

For some time Almut had been interested in more active participation in the Vauban story, but was not ready to join the thrusting and political Forum Vauban. Now she is a leading light in the successor organisation, the Vauban District Association. The story of these two organisations is in a way the lightning rod of the polarisation of opinion today about whether Vauban represents the future of green community life or is another story of how radical green grassroots action inevitably becomes co-opted into a more mainstream agenda.

The full account of the early days of resident representation is still available from the Forum Vauban archive (Forum Vauban, n.d.). The story began when the city of Freiburg decided to buy the whole of the area from the regional (or Federal) authority of Baden Württemberg. It paid €20 million for the land and, with it, responsibility for planning and development.

Instead of top-down planning, the city looked for a more experimental style of land development which became known locally as 'Learning while Planning'. This allowed the flexibility that came from a new idea to release small plots of land for new buildings between and around the standing barracks. This left the city to negotiate with other parties seeking to retrofit the military structures for residential use. It was also anticipated that more involved citizen participation (that went far beyond the legal requirements for consultation) might take some pressure off a council that had its hands full with other projects.

People started to come together as Forum Vauban during 1994, and the city formally set up a citizens association (Forum Vauban e.V.) framework in 1995. It hoped that this would co-ordinate and link dialogue and participation of local people with the master planning and other permissions that were being put together by the city planners. Membership of the Forum was made up not just from prospective residents. Many were from the university and activists from all over the city and beyond who volunteered to be part of something that was potentially going to establish a new model for European living. This atmosphere was both creative and occasionally chaotic. The Forum immediately rejected its brief restricting it to organising and commenting on the masterplan and started to produce its own ideas on how to plan and build in the district. The broad plan was finalised in 1996 and details that began to attract attention such as the car segregation policy followed over the next few years.

The first residents moved into the renovated barracks buildings in 1999. This was the SUSI or Die Selbstorganisierte Unabhängige Siedlungsinitiative. Translated as 'The Self-organised Independent Settlement Initiative', these residents had lobbied for the barracks buildings to be preserved instead of demolished and had been champions for housing for the low-paid. They believed that the freeing of valuable land by departing occupying armies should yield a social dividend for the city and should not be offered to the private sector. The first phase of the new-build programme development was completed in the following year.

In those four frenetic years between 1996 and 2000 the Forum organised over 40 workshops and excursions, held three festivals and co-ordinated a major international conference called 'UrbanVisions' in Berlin. They covered a diverse number of topics including renewable technologies, green roofs and water conservation, and the design of green spaces. They also ran workshops on many practical aspects of self-build using sustainable materials, how to finance local building projects and how to set up and run housing co-operatives. They produced a magazine called *Vauban Actuel* and always sent representatives to the Gemeinderätliche Arbeitsgruppe Vauban (the city council's Vauban committee) and other meetings of the main city council where they spoke up for local people.

Most observers and participants would say that the main achievement of the Forum was the encouragement and support they offered to Baugruppen. Even though the city produced the statutory sustainability guidelines, this still needed to be put into practice, with materials and skills sourced from providers from all over the country. Other problems were solved with local ingenuity. This epitomised the 'Learning while Planning' philosophy. The Forum was also effective with some good old-fashioned grassroots protesting, saving the famous Building 037 from being taken over by the council and eventually organising for it to be restored to be the home of Cafe Süden, which is the social centrepiece of the market square.

However, in 2004, Forum Vauban was forced to close. It ran out of money after the European Union demanded partial repayment of a grant. After a protracted legal battle a judge concluded that the funding problem was not the community's fault, but nevertheless it never returned to the original levels of energy and creativity again.

Almut says that the loss of Forum Vauban meant that there was a lot less new activity in the area and the dynamism seemed to go out of the place. Now the focus is on infrastructure and maintaining the area, in effect, a more conventional resident association role. In some ways she thinks this may have been inevitable because there is no land left for innovative sustainable projects.

Instead they still organise workshops and games and liaise with the district community worker to ensure the well-being of all of the residents. Almut is dedicated to keep the vitality of Vauban going and thinks that, while new developments may have tailed off, the district still should be proud of its achievements. She is still happy to be a guide to the busloads of eco-tourists and students who flock to the area every year.

When asked if Vauban justifies the label of 'most sustainable community in Europe', she says that everyone is still struggling to live up to that expectation.' Perhaps we don't deserve the label any more,' she says, after some reflection, but she thinks the sacrifice of those who originally established the district should serve as an inspiration for the next wave of activists who will do even better things in the future.

Perhaps unsurprisingly, not everyone is enamoured by the Vauban story. Some who live in other parts of Freiburg have been known to actively shun the community because they regard them as having a loftier opinion of their lifestyles then those living around them. The younger, perhaps more non-conformist outlook can grate with some from a more traditional south-west German perspective and there is a feeling from some that the whole 'green city' message has a whiff of the Vauban tail wagging the Freiburg dog.

Sustainable Freiburg in perspective?

Samuel is a researcher who has worked with the University of Freiburg's Institute for Environmental Social Sciences and Geography. He researches urban governance in general and the justification of city and regional claims to sustainability in particular. As an academic, but also as a resident and keen cyclist, his personal belief is that the natural surroundings of a place have a lot to do with its residents' affinity to nature. There are the cool east–west winds which announce the change of the seasons as they blow down the valley. The steep sloping undeveloped hills that rise up to the south and east of the city providing stunning views over the city and into France. This offers an expansive view of the world for those happy to make the climb away from their urban surroundings.

And then there is the evocative running water underneath the streets. These culverted watercourses, known as 'Bächle', run between the road and the pavement in many of the city centre streets and were used over past centuries for both the supply of water and to fight fires. Regeneration planners in the 1980s realised their heritage and aesthetic value as well as their ability to cool the immediate area in the summer, but the acoustic effects often have the most beneficial impact on those moving through the city centre.

Positively Responsible, a book I wrote with the organisational psychologist Cary Cooper (Bichard and Cooper, 2008), delved into the potential for Nature to influence human behaviour. Accounts explain how natural surroundings can advance healing, cause troubled young people to re-evaluate their sense of worth and inspire executives to question their role and their corporate values.

The need to preserve and protect beautiful surroundings would indeed be a plausible motivator for the citizens of Freiburg to adopt sustainable policies that go beyond other German municipalities. However, the city does not corner the market in this regard, and its arch-rival in claims to be the sustainable capital of Germany is Münster, situated on a plain near the Dutch border. While it is a very pleasant town, it cannot claim spectacular scenery as its inspiration. However, as both Samuel and Almut both cite Nature as a contributory factor to the way the city reacted to a threat, this influence could be at least part of the context in which sustainable acts are committed and should be acknowledged.

Samuel argues that the roots of the Vauban story did not grow underneath the suburb, but started in nearby Rieselfeld to the north of the more famous district. Discussions were taking place in the early 1990s about some of the city's problem neighbourhoods like Vauban and how to plan for new ones like Rieselfeld. Because money was tight, there was talk of instigating self-funding mechanisms and serviced plots to overcome the huge public investment that would be required to create these new neighbourhoods. If the city could be at least partly developed by individuals and co-operatives which could in turn attract private investors, then this would take the pressure off the public purse.

Originally, the planners came up with fairly conventional ideas about how the new districts of Rieselfeld and Vauban could be developed. But the policy developments of 1986 and the lure of new European investment funds for green development made them pause for thought. The successful application for Environment Capital status added to this and, Samuel claims, the agenda became transformed so that everything that had already happened or was about to happen was geared to sell the story of Freiburg as a sustainable icon. When the mayor started to talk up the city's green credentials, everything else fell into line.

Samuel explained that the land at Rieselfeld had previously been covered by filtration beds (the literal English translation of Rieselfeld is sewage works). The works became redundant when a larger plant was built elsewhere. Some of the site was devoted to the creation of a nature park, and the rest was zoned to accommodate a rapidly rising demand for housing at the end of the 1980s and early 1990s. Freiburg had begun to attract higher-end manufacturing businesses into what was a predominantly agriculture-based economy and workers were needed for the factories. The new district of Rieselfeld would support 4,200 housing units, eventually adding 12,000 people to the population of the city.

The planning guidelines for the area were in place by 1994, a full two years ahead of Vauban. The guidelines had all the hallmarks of a sustainable suburb. They included plans for joint design work with residents that considered the needs of families, the disabled and the elderly. It required plenty of open space both between and within residential blocks and made provision for low-carbon energy consumption. This was achieved through high insulation specifications and district heating networks powered by a combined heat and power plant and supplemented by solar electric generation. Samuel points out that while the technical and spatial elements of the scheme were largely fulfilled, the public and resident participation never really materialised during the planning stage.

The district design was the subject of an ideas competition as early as 1991. Eventually the city agreed to allow multiple small plot designs to go forward although they needed to conform to a strict design guide. Samuel explains that the whole thing was an experiment in new town development. By 2008, the tenure split was about 40 per cent each for owner occupiers (including some self-build) and rented homes, with the rest being social housing funded by private investors (Purvis, 2008). Today Rieselfeld is a pleasant enough modern suburb but has a high-density, antiseptic feel that might have been avoided if more attention had been paid to the social sustainability of the district at the beginning. There is now an active Rieselfeld Citizens Association, which can attract meetings of up to 200 people. They meet in the purpose-built Kultur Mediothek in Maria-von-Rudloff Platz, the main square. Samuel argues that the district is quite interesting as an experiment in urban design, but neither it, nor Vauban, could be termed a sustainable community.

Renaissance of the council estate

Weingarten is another 'new town'-type dormitory extension built 20 years earlier than Rieselfeld in the 1960s. The area is characterised by high-rise housing units, of which about 80 per cent were flats designed to be managed by social landlords. Today this function is performed by the Freiburger Stadtbau GmbH housing company which has around 15,000 tenants, many of them from different ethnic origins. After 30 years, the buildings needed to be renovated and the Stadtbau wanted to raise rents to pay for this, a proposal that was met with heavy opposition from the tenants. This argument coincided with a number of developments including the rise of Green Party members within the city council. By this time they had won the mayoral race in 2002 and the Party was looking to make its mark on the city.

In 1992, Freiburg's building design standards were amended to require that all new houses built on city land (or land sold by the city) should use no more than 65 kilowatt-hours of heating energy per square metre per year. This compared to the national standard of 75 kWh. The claim to be ahead of the curve was so effective that when the federal government tightened the standard some years later, Freiburg did the same to ensure that the city always stayed one step ahead of other administrations.

Back in Weingarten, the tenants organised themselves into a residents group called Forum Weingarten and negotiated improvements in return for the rent increase. Samuel maintains that the city got the message that it needed green living exemplars and, in any case, everything needed to conform to the new energy standards. Unsurprisingly a significant part of the negotiations revolved around energy-efficiency improvements to external walls and replacement windows as well as improvements to common areas. This lowered the occupation costs for tenants but the rent increases moved the gains back to where they started. Still, the move avoided net increases in living costs for the tenants and this kept the peace. Forum Weingarten was also successful in asking for the re-routing of traffic, more cycle lanes and better playground facilities. The explanation that the start of Freiburg's 'green revolution' was based on avoiding a rent strike was not something that surfaced very often after that.

Work started on the first phase in 1992 and continued until its completion in 2005. The next phase concentrated on a number of 1960s and 1970s tower blocks on the outer fringes of the district. This work is still going on today and, under the watchful eye of the still energetic members of the Forum, is perhaps the most radical work that is taking place to date. The tower known as Buggi 50 (Bugginger Straße 50) is now the first residential high-rise block to be retrofitted to Passiv-house standards. It is planned to achieve a 78 per cent reduction in energy consumption compared to its original performance. This is mainly achieved by fitting insulating cladding to the entire outer wall of the building. The design includes the enclosure of the existing inefficient balconies and the addition of new external balconies as well as modernising all of the internal services and systems. The €12 million price tag was covered by changing the space divisions, thus increasing the rentable units from 90 to 135, an average increase from six to nine flats per floor.

Prior to completion, work began on a second nearby building and some of the residents have taken up flats in the newly completed Buggi 50. Owing to the complexity in allocating space, the city appointed a community worker to help settle new residents. This proved to be so effective in avoiding disputes and helping to introduce people from different ethnic backgrounds that the worker was retained and her salary is now paid willingly by Forum Weingarten. The worker operates out of purpose-built community space on the ground floor of the building which also hosts a number of activities and leisure classes.

The grounds around the apartment are also being used for communal activities, including outdoor gyms and fruit and vegetable gardens. There were other social innovations. To ensure that all residents received equal representation, each floor had a responsible person who helped everyone to adapt to living in the newly fitted building. Learning how to operate a 'Passiv-house' flat with its restricted openings to the outside world and its internal ventilation system was one of the first hurdles that these trained floor monitors needed to overcome. Permission to display the 'Nein Danke' anti-nuclear sign was another. The building took a vote and a good majority of the residents thought that it was right for residents to advertise their anti-nuclear allegiance if that is what they wanted to do.

It would be easy to write glowing and uncompromisingly positive accounts of the Buggi process, but Samuel counsels against a total embrace of the scheme. First, like many retrofit projects, almost all of the original tenants of Buggi 50 have not returned to live in the building. After three years out of their homes, many found accommodation elsewhere and were reluctant to move again within such a short space of time. Another issue is the community meeting space which is unlikely to be provided in the next three building projects. The scheme is also cutting many of the new external balconies because they are too expensive to fit.

Samuel says that the exhaustive community consultation that was carried out before Buggi 50 has not been repeated in subsequent phases and even the lush green Tramway that runs past the buildings is not what it seems. Samuel says that the city is fond of pointing out that the grassy tramway (where green growth pokes through semi-permeable mesh) is a further example of the (literally) green city. The truth is that this is a noise suppression measure and just happens to look nice. Samuel's points are not made to find fault in the overall sustainability accomplishments of the city. He just feels that not all of the decisions were taken for purely environmental reasons. Politics, opportunistic bids for funding and expediency all played a part in the green reputation of Freiburg. While Vauban is still being pushed forward as the poster settlement for sustainable living, it was arguably Rieselfeld that was the forerunner of the green settlement and Weingarten that is now innovating on sustainable built environment solutions. But the presence of a radical group of green activists thrust the former barracks to the fore and the rest is history.

Co-operation is the key

Martin and Peter (name changed on request) were involved in setting up the Genova housing co-operative in Vauban. They have been part of a rich understanding about the history, context and the direction of travel of the district. Peter was a city administrator, but after doing a Master's degree he became interested in community energy. After time spent in Austria doing a PhD, he returned to Freiburg to teach in local schools. He says his passions lay in the realms of environmental governance and he has always maintained an interest in living lightly on the land with the lowest ecological footprint possible. Martin is a physicist who moved into environmental sciences and spent time in Berlin before moving to Freiburg. He also went into school teaching (physics) in secondary schools and before becoming interested in co-operative living, he had been active in the anti-nuclear movement and was a member of the Green Party.

When the new eco-districts of Rieselfeld and Vauban were announced, both men wanted to become involved. As the development of Rieselfeld was ahead of Vauban, they both tried to influence the design and the level of citizen participation during the planning phase. They found the city planners were not receptive to their ideas and failed to make any impact on the eventual outcome of the district. Far from being discouraged, when the opportunity to get involved in Vauban arose, they tried again and were both founder members of Forum Vauban.

Having learned from their experience in Rieselfeld, they set about influencing the council in a more effective manner. When invited to agree with Samuel's analysis that much of what has happened in Freiburg was essentially green-wash, both deny that this was the case. However, they do recall that the administration was reluctant to put Vauban forward for the Istanbul UN Habitat conference as a model city. Their recollection is that the mayor was swayed by the promise of EU funding on the back of the profile the city would get for appearing at the conference.

By the time Vauban was being planned, there were a few pro-environment politicians on the city council and Martin and Peter (along with many others) lobbied them heavily to put the case for a sustainable suburb. They argued that this needed to include a generous amount of low-income housing to ensure social sustainability. They had plenty of allies for this, including the SUSI group. One of the key issues was how much land the council would put up for sale and how much would be made available to the housing for rent sector. Another was the idea that cars should be excluded from much of the district. While the campaign to exclude cars was a success, the battle to secure large amounts of rented space and limit land offered to the private spec-ulators could only be claimed as a partial victory. Eventually they took mat-ters into their own hands and decided to form a housing co-operative themselves. The idea started from a concept that originated in East Germany called shared equity, designed to cater for people who were unable to get a loan to buy a property outright.

Both men were excited about the catalytic effect that Forum Vauban was having on both its members and on the city council. One year after floating the idea of setting up the housing co-operative in the Forum, they had attracted over 80 members. This posed problems as they realised that every-one would need a role and a stake in the management of the group if they were to continue to keep their interest and support. The next challenge was finance. They managed to raise about half of the money they needed to build their first building from the membership, but the rest had to come from the bank. They had very big ambitions but the financial situation enabled them to construct only two buildings. Once the construction was completed and the first tenants had moved in, they found that there was far more demand than they had anticipated and Phase 2 started to be planned almost immediately.

By this time, the money-raising challenges were more complex and they had to concede that it was necessary to allow some of the first-phase occu-pants to buy their houses in order to finance the next phase. This proved to be a divisive move as it created a two-tier membership between the owners and the renters. They managed this process by maintaining an active dialogue and encouraging mixing between the two types of occupants. By 2001, the co-operative had built four buildings, of four storeys each, containing 73 flats. To com-pensate for the small units, they built common rooms and guest rooms where visitors could stay. The second phase also incorporated business and office space which gave the co-operative some additional income.

A further challenge was to try to keep rents down in order to ensure that the co-operative could continue to serve low-income tenants. Now they are thinking about a third phase, but there is worry within the membership that the co-operative will become too big and people will cease to know each other well. After 15 years, Genova seems to have reached the limit of growth, not because of financial issues but because of social pressures from within.

When asked if the Vauban project has been completed, they offer a mixed analysis. They can see that there are more cars parked around the periphery of the car-free zone, and unfortunately many of them are large SUVs. Prices have increased markedly for the private renters and the innovation that surrounded development in the area is no longer in evidence because the land has run out. They think the main mistake was when the city gave too much land (40 per cent) to private developers. If the Baugruppen and co-operatives had been allowed to dominate the area, they do not think that the slow creeping influx of affluent residents from outside the area would have occurred. That is not to say that they believe in creating low-income ghettos, and they argue that the Genova model works because of the mixture of people on different incomes and from different backgrounds. But the two give off a real sense that the deeper green values are seeping out of the area.

Martin and Peter also regret the reputation of Vauban as being an insular society. There is the worry that even though there has been a socio-economic shift, this perception is not going away. The original alternative lifestyle that was frowned upon by some is being replaced by a different clique of highly educated professionals. This wasn't what they signed up for when they started their project. They are intensely proud of their achievements and feel their end has held up very well. The co-operative is thriving and their concern when we met was how they were going to re-decorate the community room without upsetting people who still remembered the children who chose the materials for the original murals 15 years ago. Looking back, they are particularly keen to point out that they did not receive any external help either to raise the funds for their development or to build it.

They can also point to some useful spin-offs of their ideas. One of these is the setting up in 2011 of GartenCoop Freiburg. The 260-strong membership forms partnerships with farmers by offering labour and distribution in return for a share of the crops. The organic produce is, they say, a reaction against climate change and the predicted end of domination by fossil fuels both in the energy mix and as the mainstay of agro-business and the food chain. They apply the same sustainable convictions to the food co-op as they did when they set up Genova.

It is perhaps inevitable that the legend of Vauban cannot stand up to every element of scrutiny. But it is unfair and inaccurate to say that it does not deserve its reputation either. Freiburg continues to be a popular relocation city for many Germans and there is still close to a 20,000-unit housing shortage which is forcing rents up across all areas. It was perhaps over-ambitious to ever think that the whole of the district would be made up of Passiv-houses powered by sewage, but there is still a very impressive number of low-energy houses concentrated in one place.

On the city-wide scale, there was the failure to meet the self-imposed target of a 25 per cent drop in greenhouse gas emissions by 2010, mainly because of the national switch away from nuclear power. Now there is a new target of 40 per cent less CO_2 by 2030. And despite all the emphasis on reducing the influence of climate change, the city can only claim that around 4 per cent of the electricity comes from self-generated renewable sources. There is also grumbling from groups like Friends of the Earth that the city burns too much of its refuse and, because of inefficient technology, it has been de-coupled from its energy from waste plant, making it even more unsustainable. A new biomass-fired power plant has not placated the group.

But even these shortcomings can be balanced by high employment in green jobs, particularly in the thriving solar energy sector adding, so the city claims, some €650 million to the local economy. The city now hosts an impressive number of sustainable bodies, including the Eco-Institute's Office, the European Office of ICLEI (Local Governments for Sustainability), the Fraunhofer Institute for Solar Energy Systems and the International Solar Energy Society.

Vauban has wagged the dog in some respects. The way that road traffic was handled in the district was so impressive that the city changed the by-laws that restrict on-street parking in many other areas. Vauban's early adoption of renewable CHP (combined heat and power with an energy mix of 80 per cent wood chips and 20 per cent natural gas) has influenced the rest of the city which now boasts that 50 per cent of its electricity is from CHP, though much of this is gas-fired. Vauban's impressive collection of solar electric arrays has led to a city-wide count of more than 400 photovoltaic installations, including a tourist-drawing expanse on the roof of the city's football stadium.

All these gains, it could be argued, stem from the halcyon period in the early 1990s when a group of idealistic people thought that it could be possible to build a truly sustainable community. It may or may not matter that the context to allow these 'dreams' was created from motives that were less than sustainable, but the fact that Vauban exists and is still providing inspiration is testament to the will of those people who made it work and the enduring power of collective community action.

3 The anti-frackers

Unconventional opposition to unconventional gas

The next environmental battleground

In May 2012, the International Energy Agency (IEA) issued a special report on the exploitation of shale gas called *Golden Rules for a Golden Age of Gas* (IEA, 2012). The IEA press release argued that the report treated 'with equal seriousness' the excitement of a new fossil fuel energy source and the anxieties that this might cause severe damage to global social and environmental interests. The report presented the way forward for what it interpreted as the responsible exploitation of the new resource. It also painted a picture of what would happen if the 'tide turns' and constraints against shale gas meant that extraction proved to be impossible.

The potential for shale gas to dominate the fossil market in coming years is striking. The IEA report says that gas, as a proportion of overall global energy use, could grow from 14 per cent to 32 per cent by 2035 if these new 'unconventional' reserves are tapped. This rise would leave gas as the second most used energy source behind oil, although the IEA projection put oil, gas and coal at broadly equal volumes at this time. But it warns that under-utilisation of shale gas could lead to a 1.3 per cent increase in greenhouse gases because oil and coal (with their higher carbon intensities) would have to be used in its place. In other words, shale gas needs to be exploited to lessen the impact of global warming – it's a good thing. Committed readers need to go past the executive summary and soldier on until the 90th page before the report concedes that if shale gas reserves were fully exploited, it would mean that global warming would increase to at least 3.5°C, well past the current target of 2°C.

The science regarding the implications of global warming is becoming more and more certain, but because of the complexity of the global systems, the difference between 2°C and 3.5°C is not always clear to many people. The fact that the IEA considered it necessary to produce the report at all was due at least in part to the high-profile opposition to shale gas exploitation put up by local objectors and in part to a few notable decisions to ban its exploitation in some areas around the world. The most graphic explanation can been seen in what is known now as the 'burning ember' diagram, so called because the sliding scale of risk moved from white (low risk) through orange and then red (high risk). This was produced by the authors of the *Third Assessment Report of the Intergovernmental Panel on Climate Change* (McCarthy *et al*., 2001).

The diagram plots risk levels against five 'reasons for concern' that would arise if global warming increased. These include risks to unique and threatened ecosystems (coral reefs, endangered species, etc.), risks from extreme weather events, risks that some areas may be worse affected than others, risks of multiple impacts in the same place (cost of recovery, fatalities, infrastructure interruption, etc.) and risks from large-scale events such as the collapse of the west Antarctic or Greenland ice sheets. When the burning ember diagram was updated in 2009 (Smith *et al*., 2009), it showed that if the world heats up beyond 3°C, all five reasons for concern will be in the red.

On this evidence, there is a substantial concern that the exploitation of any new fossil fuel resources would represent a threat to global systems. However, the industry is putting forward a coherent 'least bad' counter-argument for shale gas which is gaining traction in some quarters. This requires a further layer of the issue to be uncovered. Most people are familiar with the fact that fossil fuels (oil, coal and gas) occur in deposits deep in the ground or under the sea bed. Typically these deposits are concentrated in one place and once a hole is drilled, the oil and gas can be pumped out and refined for use. Over recent decades, the depletion of easily reached reserves and the increase in demand from a growing number of industrialising countries have made previously expensive sources of energy in hard-to-reach places or hard-to-refine forms more economically attractive. One example is the oil tar reserves in Alberta, Canada. These are typically sands that are coated in a viscous form of hydrocarbon often referred to as tar or bitumen.

The surface or strip-mine excavation of these reserves attracted widespread condemnation from national and international environmental groups such as Greenpeace and the Sierra Club, as well as some concerned businesses like Patagonia and the Co-operative Bank in the UK. However, while this activity was a concern for dedicated protesters, it did not take off as a global *cause célèbre*. This may have been because the concentrations of the deposits mainly occur in a remote part of Canada. In addition, more eye-catching environmental disasters, notably the Deepwater Horizon oil spill into the Gulf of Mexico, have helped to divert attention from the area.

Why, then, has the opposition to shale gas exploitation gained so much more of a global notoriety, particularly when new jobs and the substitution of oil and coal with gas are apparently an attractive option? The answer lies partly in where the deposits are found and partly in how the gas is taken from the ground. While the hydrocarbon in the tar sands is thick and viscous, tiny bubbles of natural gas can also occur in rock formed from deposits of silt and mud that become compressed into rock known as shale. Shale gas is not a new phenomenon. The first wells in the USA were drilled in 1821 near Fredonia in New York State (Haszeldine, 2011). Like tar sands, the resource was available, but could not be exploited as cheaply as oil and coal. However, some adherents persevered and worked on more efficient ways to extract the gas. At times, such as the oil crisis of the 1970s and again in the 1980s, this work was more economically attractive and made shale gas and other 'unconventional' sources such as tight sandstones and coal seams worth the investment. Politically, cheap sources of energy were and still are important, but so too was avoiding the dependence on foreign energy.

Almost half of the gas-bearing shale deposits in the USA lies in what is known as the Marcellus shale beds. 'Frac Focus', the US national hydraulic fracturing chemical registry (http://www.fracfocus.org/) shows that there are now over 2,200 registered shale gas wells drilled in the Marcellus beds, although opponents say that figure is closer to 6,000. The huge stratum varies in depth and lies under large parts of Pennsylvania, overlapping into western parts of New York State and Maryland and eastern parts of West Virginia and Ohio. Pennsylvania bears the brunt of the drilling activity. While there are some wells in Ohio and West Virginia, they represent less than 10 per cent of those drilled thus far. New York State has, since 2008, placed a moratorium on drilling while more research is carried out. Opposition in New York State is active and has celebrity support and so it is unlikely that widespread activity will take place there for the foreseeable future. A *de facto* moratorium is in place in Maryland until 2014.

Exploiting the resource depends on the ability to split apart or fracture the dense rock, thus freeing the trapped gas. Typically, vertical wells are drilled into the shale deposits. This process often penetrates potable water aquifers which should be protected by steel or cement well casings. When it reaches the shale beds, the drill direction is changed from vertical to horizontal. This can create a well or tunnel stretching over 1,000 metres long. Depending on the geological structures, the well can be directed toward existing faults or cracks in the shale which can make extraction easier as it offers a natural pathway for gas to escape into the well. However, this can also trigger earthquakes as witnessed in Ohio in December 2011 and Lancashire in England in April and May earlier that year.

The next stage of the extraction process involves the segmentation of the well. Sections of the casing are perforated, and the hydraulic fracturing or 'fracking' is initiated. Fracking is the process whereby large volumes of pressurised water, sand and proprietary chemicals are injected into the rock. The pressure fractures the shale and the sand props open fissures, enabling the gas to flow out of the rock and out into the well.

Academics, regulators and protesters point to a range of impacts (both environmental and socio-economic) that they believe make this process unacceptable. There are a number of concerns about the pollution of both surface water and groundwater sources and about soil contamination as a result of the leakages of process water into areas adjacent to the well and the platform site.

Once the fracking process has commenced, millions of litres of water contaminated with a range of chemicals needs to be pumped back out of the wells and either sent by tanker to a licensed facility or treated on-site. Organisations such as ProPublica, an independent group of investigative journalists (www.propublica.org), have reported extensively on the negative implications of this, and researchers in the USA have found that the wells could be causing natural salt to migrate through the rock to contaminate freshwater aquifers (Warner *et al.*, 2012),

Frac Focus lists dozens of chemicals that are injected into the shale gas wells. These are used as viscosity controllers, lubricants, gelling agents and emulsifiers. The chemicals include acids, chlorides, hydrocarbons such as methanol and ethylene glycol and biocides such as glutaraldehyde. Missing from the Frac Focus list are so-called BTEX compounds including benzene (a human carcinogen) and toluene. A report by Democratic Party members of the Congressional Committee on Energy and Commerce (2011) said that these were regularly used by the fracking industry in 2011.

The report stated that 14 leading oil and gas service companies had, at the time the report was produced, injected 780 million gallons of hydraulic fracturing products into the water used for fracking. This included more than 2,500 hydraulic fracturing products containing 750 different chemicals and other components. The US Environmental Protection Agency has yet to definitively link contaminated water surrounding fracking sites with leaks from the drilling process. In the UK, the Department of Energy and Climate Change has given a cautious agreement for drilling to continue, provided volumes of fracking liquids are reduced and flow-back is reclaimed promptly to avoid seismic activity (DECC, 2012a). In June 2012, New Jersey, the state that borders Pennsylvania, approved a law banning the treatment or storage of fracking waste (Navarro, 2012a).

The other main concern surrounding fracking is the release of greenhouse gases. The industry and some political supporters laud the exploitation of natural gas for the jobs it creates, the (potentially) lower energy prices that will result from abundant gas and the improvement in fuel security as foreign oil imports are reduced. But they are also talking up the improvement in greenhouse gas emissions because the combustion of natural gas emits almost 30 per cent less carbon dioxide than oil and just under 45 per cent less than coal (IEA, 2012).

However, a team from Cornell University reported that extracting natural gas from the Marcellus shale beds could do more to aggravate global warming than mining coal (Howarth *et al.*, 2011). The work centred on the extraction process and showed that methane leaking into the atmosphere during hydraulic fracturing could offset any gains from replacing more carbon-intensive forms of energy. The researchers explain that methane is a much more potent greenhouse gas than carbon dioxide, especially in the short term, with 105 times more warming impact, and is 20 times more effective at retaining heat in the atmosphere over a 100-year period (EPA, 2012).

The work compared estimated CO_2 emissions for shale gas, conventional gas, coal (surface-mined and deep-mined) and diesel oil. They concluded that as much as 8 per cent of the methane in shale gas leaks into the air during the lifetime of the well. This is approximately two times the amount that leaks from a conventional gas production well. The implication of this is that shale gas is not only worse for climate change than conventional gas, but it is also worse than oil. The authors were careful to say that they were not arguing for more coal or oil, but the work suggested that this method of gas production could have environmental consequences (Howarth *et al.*, 2011). There are two reasons why shale gas leaks more methane than other forms of fossil fuel extraction. One is the depth and complexity of the operation, resulting in more time taken to drill a shale gas well. The other is that it requires the withdrawal of fluids (or 'flow back' as it is called), which leads to extended periods of venting.

The Marcellus Protest

The north-east United States is the birthplace of unconventional gas, so it is not surprising to find that considerable efforts to oppose it can be found in the heartland of the Marcellus shale beds in Pennsylvania. However, there are many other parts of the world where reserves have been found and drillers are drilling. Almost every one of them has a matching anti-fracking group tracking their every move. The IEA report states that main areas of interest outside the USA are Canada, Mexico, China, Australia and parts of Europe. Only a few places outside North America have produced anything but promise to date. China's first shale gas pilot programme started in Liangping County in south-western China's Chongqing municipality in the autumn of 2012 (*China Daily*, 2012).

Poland and France have the largest gas-bearing shale depots in Europe, but while the former is an enthusiastic supporter of shale gas exploitation, France (along with the Czech Republic and Bulgaria) has banned all drilling. The UK has two separate deposits that could be commercially significant but activity is still at the exploration phase. One occurs in the north-west of England, while the other lies under some counties south of London.

In the USA, stories about the damage fracking does to individual land-owners and farmland in Pennsylvania started to spread on the internet and opposition to the exploration companies' actions started to grow. Some towns and settlements invoked local zoning legislation to ensure that the drilling platforms were sited well away from housing. However, in 2011, the state agreed with the gas companies that this was a confusing and haphazard arrangement and passed a law known as Act 13. This overrode all local zoning laws and allowed drilling to occur up to 300 feet from buildings in all cases, regardless of local conditions. To assuage the outcry against this, Act 13 also required the gas companies to pay a per-well fee to the affected councils and overhauled the state environmental rules.

The new law was quickly challenged by those who argued that it took control away from voters who had struggled hard for their local decision-making rights. In July 2012, the Commonwealth (of Pennsylvania) Court agreed with them and ruled that the zoning part of Act 13 was unconstitutional. The ruling said that the state's requirement allowed 'incompatible uses in zoning districts', failed to protect the interests of neighbouring property owners and altered the character of neighbourhoods (Navarro, 2012b). The 'impact fees' levied on the gas companies to mitigate the environmental problems (including road damage, water and soil contamination, etc.) have started to come through with 75 per cent going to the local authorities and the rest to the state.

In July 2010, a group of individuals and organisations came together to pool their resources in a common fight against the expansion of shale gas exploration in the State of Pennsylvania. Calling themselves the Marcellus Protest, the group came together from a position of strength as many had already been active prior to its formation. Marking the group's two-year anniversary, their newsletter declared:

> The first phase of involvement, 'awareness', has gone quickly. Now, the struggle becomes harder; the vested interests are responding to us as a threat. We're shouted-down by demonization, disinformation, and deliberate confusion. They have money; they will buy what they need: publicity, politicians, and even academics. But we're 2! And we're getting bigger and stronger.

Most of the membership of the Marcellus Protest lives in and around urban Pittsburgh. While much of the drilling to date has occurred in rural and wooded areas to the east of the city, the thirst for potential assets took the gas exploration companies right up to the outskirts of urban Pittsburgh and that was the cue for a very effective green community action to come together.

Many members of the group could not call themselves life-long environmentalists although there are a number of well-informed individuals trained in natural sciences among their number. The common themes for Marcellus Protest members are fairness and justice (both social and environmental). They spend long hours discussing ways to challenge what they see as the misinformation and obfuscation that the industry and their supporting politicians are feeding to the media. They look not only at whether the facts are right, but also how the issue is framed. They have seen how the arguments for continuing with the drilling are justified by the creation of jobs, the supply of cheap energy and the guarantee that lights in the homes and factories in the state will stay on if they are allowed to continue.

Claudia and John live in the Squirrel Hill district of Pittsburgh. It's a nice neighbourhood with tree-lined streets on steep sloping hills, typical of many of the outlying districts of the city. They are both retired now but are far from inactive. Claudia worked for a women's drug addiction charity and has always been an activist in the women's rights movement since the 1970s. In retirement she volunteered to help out at a single-parent project and it was there that she first came across the issue of fracking. One of the women that she was working with invited her to an event and she went along to hear what the speakers had to say. Little did she realise that this would be the start of a journey that would lead her to press her Senator about the safeguards he should be lobbying to enforce to keep the shale gas industry from damaging state water and land.

Claudia still does not really consider herself to be an environmentalist. And while the couple are active in the Christian community, she does not claim this as a driving motivation either, apart from the broad affinity Christians have for natural justice. Her experience of protest groups before joining the Marcellus Protest was limited to human rights and anti-torture campaigns. But the shale gas issue pushed her into activism and her motivation came from the deep dissatisfaction and disappointment with the political processes that were supposed to protect the population. She was moved to stand in the way of what she saw as individual corrupt elements, both within politics and the corporate sector.

When she started analysing the statements that the industry was making and looked in detail at some of the politicians' assurances, she became very sceptical about the quality of information that the public was receiving. The more she looked into their claims, the more she knew that they were not telling the truth. She started writing letters to the editor of the *Pittsburgh Post-Gazette* pointing out these inaccuracies and had a few letters published. Encouraged, she started her own email list and sent more detailed information pieces to the local newspapers. These longer missives were less successful although to be fair at that time (2008–9), the issue was just emerging. Now the *Post-Gazette* covers the issue on almost a daily basis.

Claudia's 23-page paper on the employment claims of the industry called 'Jobs and Community Benefits: Deconstructing Gas Industry "Messaging"' is a good example of the care she took over her research (Detwiler, 2011). Her opening paragraph states:

> In a depressed economy, promises of jobs and economic benefits are unbeatable as a way to defuse critical review of exploitation of a resource. The gas drilling industry has counted on these carefully constructed messages of abundance to discourage serious conversation about the damage to individual, environmental, and community health.

She also cites the work of others, such as the Pennsylvania Budget and Policy Center, which noted that communication by the consortia of shale gas producers

> overstates the number of jobs supported by the industry. It states that 140,000 jobs are supported … but jobs data from the State Department of Labor and Industry show that less than 19,000 people were employed directly in core Marcellus Shale industries at the end of 2010.
>
> (PBPC, 2011)

As Claudia got deeper into the subject, she felt that a more organised approach was needed to challenge the shale gas industry, but she was reluctant to be the co-ordinator of such an effort. She felt that she had spent a working lifetime setting up and running organisations and would have preferred others to take the lead. She did join an outreach committee of other interested individuals that had started in the city and decided to attempt a limited project in an area where she had connections.

The operation to secure a land bank for potential exploration by the drilling companies had, to the later dismay of their communications teams, extended to church land, including graveyards. Claudia realised that she could use her connections to lobby her church, and perhaps other denominations, to call a moratorium on fracking on their land. The lobbying effort led her to speak to congregations and ministers and later, through the Marcellus Protest, to speak to other groups who had expressed an interest in the subject. This new role as spokesperson happened almost by accident as she had originally agreed just to co-ordinate volunteer speakers but found that she knew more than some of the people who came forward.

By this time, Claudia was joined by her husband John who came to the Protest from another direction. John is a retired engineer who specialised in automating processes in heavy industry. He looks back on his career with pride in his professional competency but regrets that some of the work he did led to environmental impacts in areas such as the steel industry. Like Claudia, John had always risen to the challenge of social injustice and was protesting against the Vietnam War almost half a century ago. When the G20 economic summit came to Pittsburgh in 2009, a lot of protesters congregated in the city centre opposite the Convention Center to protest. People were there to express their views on a range of issues to do with economic injustice and the impact of globalisation. Because of the civil unrest that had taken place in other cities, the police over-reacted to the protesters and the media showed pictures of crowd being broken up by rounds of tear gas and concussion grenades. John was on the streets that day as part of a group of amateur documentary makers. He met many other people at this time including anti-fracking groups. Intrigued, he attended a coffeehouse meeting and, knowing that Claudia was also interested in the subject, started to follow the arguments. Because of his professional background, he was able to scrutinise what the gas industry had to say.

In November 2010, there was a gas trade exhibition at the Convention Center and a demonstration was arranged. The people who had been informally gathering up to that point wanted to organise a significant showing for this and formed what was to be the core of the Marcellus Protest. John volunteered to write content for the pamphlets that they handed out during the demonstration. Thinking about it now, he said that the way the industry was extending its influence struck him as underhand and dishonest. This offended his strong sense of logic, reason and fairness.

However, what really fired John's willingness to become an activist was the betrayal of the ethics of business he had come to believe was required of corporate leaders. The notorious story of the CEO of Chesapeake Energy (one of the leading fracking companies) was the one John says was particularly disappointing. The company is the second largest gas corporation behind Exxon Mobile in the USA. In 2008, Aubray McClendon, who was at the time both Chief Executive and Chairman of Chesapeake, was awarded a $112.5 million package, including a $75 million bonus and other perks by his board. The story was tracked and reported by journalist Ian Urbina at the *New York Times* as well as Bloomberg, Reuters and the *Pittsburgh Post-Gazette* because of the widespread interest Chesapeake had in the shale gas reserves under Pennsylvania. The award caused uproar among shareholders as the huge pay-off coincided with a 58 per cent drop in the company's stock price because of weakening gas prices, sparking a crisis in the CEO's own personal finances. It emerged later that McClendon was so desperate for money that he sold a set of antique maps to his own company for $12 million, a sum he was compelled to pay back a few years later.

Much later, in May 2011, the state fined Chesapeake more than $1 million (Pennsylvania's largest ever fine to an oil and gas company) for contaminating the water supplies of 16 families in Bradford County while drilling for shale gas. In July 2012, a Bloomberg story also revealed that for 23 years (the whole time the company had been in existence), Chesapeake had paid just $53 million in income taxes on $5.5 billion in pre-tax profits, a rate of about 1 per cent. It did this by interpreting rules that allow American oil and gas companies to delay the payment of taxes during the exploration phase. To John, this behaviour was unacceptable and deserved to be challenged.

His niche in the group is online skills and he is happy to co-ordinate and maintain the Marcellus Protest web-site, including fielding comments and questions put to the group via the info@ email address. Together, Claudia and John cannot possibly be regarded as excitable radicals who are prone to challenge the establishment. But their testimony suggests that it was the excesses of the establishment that provoked these considered and thoughtful people to take up the struggle against the frackers and politicians that support them.

Mel is in his sixties now and semi-retired. He has held down a number of jobs during his working life, including over a decade as a truck driver and a period as a nuclear medical technologist. Like a number of Marcellus Protest members, he was not particularly interested in environmental matters until some Green Party friends invited him to a meeting where the film *Gasland* was shown. The film was made in June 2010 by Josh Fox, following an approach by shale gas companies to lease his land for exploration. The memorable moment in the film comes when a Colorado resident, Mike Markham, who lives near a shale gas well, puts a lighter to his open water tap, resulting in a small fireball as the escaping methane ignites.

The industry has since tried to rebut this by citing a Colorado Oil and Gas Conservation Commission report (COGCC, n.d.) saying the gas came from naturally occurring coal measures. But the report does not explain how the fracking of a nearby well coincided with the escape of the methane into drinking water pipes and the argument over who or what is to blame continues today. This technical wrangle is lost on those watching *Gasland* who find that a flaming water tap makes for compelling and worrying viewing.

Mel was no different, and after seeing the film, he became aware of the approaches that were being made to landowners by companies for gas exploration within the Pittsburgh boundaries. He has since become well informed and articulate about the aim of these companies to leverage corporate money and increase stock prices by arguing that the land assets that they control equate to future gas reserves. While some landowners were happy to accept the payments for access, many others became suspicious and eventually the tactic backfired when the urban population of Pittsburgh became so concerned that they supported a city-wide ban.

Jessica is a botanist and works for a state agency. Her entry into the Marcellus Protest started when she volunteered for a bike project and heard about shale gas drilling through other volunteers. When it started to hit the headlines in 2010, she got together with others she knew to form an environmental group called the Shadbush Environmental Justice Collective 'that was particularly interested in looking at the links between politicians' promises and environmental impacts' (Shadbush, 2013). Although their stated aim was to avoid being tied to a single issue, their radical mission led them inexorably into opposition to shale gas exploitation. The group's stated 'points of unity' suggest a deep green influence and a marked distrust in the ability of market structures to address the damage that the existing political and economic systems are exerting on the environment. The group reaches out in solidarity to affected communities suffering from environmental impacts. The issues around shale gas had everything the group was formed to oppose. Since then, Jessica and other group members have been using a range of indirect and non-violent direct action methods to put their views across to industry and the public. They can often be found at the sites of wellheads to raise awareness and protest in support of affected residents.

While interested in protecting the operational and political independence of Shadbush, Jessica says that there is no problem in participating in the wider Marcellus Protest network. She has been amazed at the number and variety of different people who come to anti-fracking meetings. Jessica was under the impression that Pittsburgh was not a city where you would find militant or politically active people beyond the usual constituencies of, for example, unions or neighbourhood-specific campaigns. The range of backgrounds and ages coming together against shale gas in one broad group has impressed her. Shadbush is almost exclusively a young people's organisation, which benefited from members being able to drop what they were doing and join a direct action protest at short notice. But the downside was that many young people who joined at the start and went on the early protests became disillusioned when they saw that the industry was more resilient than they thought. When the drilling continued despite their best efforts, she was concerned that they would lose heart and drift away. She had seen this happen before when protest groups failed to stop strip-mining in the state after a ten-year fight.

Jessica could see that a fluctuating membership could destabilise the group. But she was equally concerned that if they merged with others, it could dilute their message and compromise their methods. The alliance with the Marcellus Protest members was a good fit in that, as a confederation rather than rigid entity, it could happily accommodate Shadbush on its own terms. Jessica and Shadbush continue with fundraisers and camps to keep their own momentum going, but respond when Marcellus Protest actions need a helping hand.

Terri has been an active civil rights and women's rights campaigner all her life. She came to hear about the shale gas issue through a friend who was an artist and had watched *Gasland* on television. It turned out that she already knew a few people who were involved in the Marcellus Protest and joined the group to try to influence a ban on drilling in her own neighbourhood. Wilkinsburg is a suburb of Pittsburgh just outside the city boundary and therefore unprotected by the city-wide ban that had recently been agreed by the council. In March 2012, with help from the Environmental Defense Fund, Terri got a unanimous vote from the Wilkinsburg councillors to prohibit drilling.

Helping to secure the ban was exhilarating, but after that victory Terri has been looking for a new role in the Protest. She signed up to be a co-ordinator and still goes to all of the events. She believes there should be a universal global ban and has been following developments in other parts of the world. She thinks that the Marcellus Protest has achieved the first wave of their objective by raising awareness and helping communities to vote for local bans. But she recognises that the Protest is at a crossroads and that it may have lost some momentum. She wonders if a Greenpeace-style stunt like dumping rubbish on the drilling platforms might do the trick. She has also considered going over the border to Ohio where activists are only just getting started on their first round of protests.

Loretta thinks that the older you get, the more you need to grow, both mentally and physically. She says that her involvement in the Marcellus Protest has helped her to do this. Ultimately it's about altruism and she believes that people need to feel that collective action will win out over injustice and stop feeling isolated and powerless. One of her earliest memories is when she stepped out into the road, to the horror of her mother, and stopped the traffic. The realisation that everyone has the ability to take individual action to make a dramatic statement had a profound effect on her. She has worked many jobs in her life and even went back to university to do a psychology degree. Her challenge of authority was learned during her experience working in a residential home for disturbed young people. She became upset and frustrated that the preferred method of treatment was medication rather than more individual support. Her confidence in management was further undermined when she was asked by the union if she would represent the workers as a shop steward. There was a push for better working conditions and she tried to get reluctant staff to sign a petition. Unsuccessful, she was later compelled to leave her job and decided to concentrate on earning a living from a number of properties she owned. It was through this route that she read a flyer that was pushed through one of her doors. It was from a gas company asking if she was interested in selling access rights to her land.

She said that this raised a red flag in her mind, particularly when she heard that Halliburton was one of the companies involved. Halliburton was the company made famous through its association with President George W. Bush's Vice President Dick Cheney. Sensitised to the issue, she went to a community meeting at Mount Lebanon library to hear a talk on fracking. They showed *Gasland*, and like others, it made her even more concerned about shale gas. She started going to other meetings both out-of-town and at the city council. Gradually she became committed to fighting against the gas companies and developed her own myth-busting fact sheet which she took to every meeting she attended.

After joining the Marcellus Protest, Loretta became much more focused on the different communications channels the group could use to get their message across. She wondered if it was possible to use radio to do this and at one point helped to develop a public information advertisement. The ad never ran because the radio station got cold feet, fearing a loss in advertising revenue. This did not deter her and on the back of the developments following Act 13, she has continued to try to get the ad on the air. Loretta could have been forgiven for being put off by confrontation after the bruising experience of losing her job at the hospital. But it seems to have had the opposite effect on her. She now believes that people need to understand success and failure if they are to realise their full potential to change things, even when it looks like the cause is futile.

Doug Shields once piloted a ship in the Gulf of Mexico serving the oil and gas industry. Ironic then that he has played such a prominent role in the fight against the frackers. A more recent and prominent job was as adviser to the Mayor of Pittsburgh. In 2004, he used that experience to become elected to the Pittsburgh City Council where he served until 2012. Doug says that all the different jobs he held down before he got elected helped him to form the perspective that he needed as a politician. He had travelled the world and had met many different kinds of people. He spent time understanding issues related to social justice and human expectations. Doug first heard about shale gas in 2003. Loretta and her partner Ken brought the land assembly issue to his attention. He said that the more he looked into fracking, the more concerned he became. He started to think about how the zoning (land use planning) code could be applied to stop the drilling in the city. He then contacted the Environmental Defense League and, together with another member of the council, he drafted a bill that, in legal terms, was based on the protection of rural land and farmers' rights. Doug could see that what was good for farmers could also work for urbanites. The bill was designed to secure the right to reject any gas exploration within the city boundary. The press became interested when they understood that the gasmen were attempting to gain rights to cemeteries. In August 2010, they tabled the bill and fielded elected members, academics and lawyers for the press conference. On 16 November, the pair successfully piloted the bill through the council with a unanimous vote in favour of the ban. The unanimity was important because it meant that even the Mayor could not veto the bill.

Talking to Doug, it's clear that getting the bill passed was one of his prouder moments. On leaving office he could have walked away from the controversy, but this issue stayed with him and he joined the Marcellus Protest to continue to work on ways to slow the progress of the shale gas industry across the state. And there have been new battles to fight, particularly the state's Act 13 which threatens to undo his local zoning victory. He thinks the Marcellus Protest will need new blood but inevitably he is not worried about this. He thinks the gas industry is their best recruiter, as new wells are drilled and more pollution and hardship lead to more protesters. His politician's eye observes that the opposition to fracking is a rare classless issue which means that neither industry nor politicians can divide and rule. It has tried to separate 'blue-collar' working people from the middle class by arguing that shale gas means more jobs. And Act 13 allows gas money to be paid to compliant townships. But the industry is having a hard time picking off protest groups made up of a diverse range of people united in opposition to the erosion of their rights, a mistrust of rich corporations and a concern that their water taps will explode.

Doug's political observations are important because as an elected official sitting in the middle of a web of popular opinion, he was able to recognise that fracking is an unusual type of single issue. Its narrow definition and diverse constituency-based protesters linked by an effective communication strategy means it is tailor-made for twenty-first-century green community action. It attracts a range of people – young and old, educated and not, rich and poor, and from a wide range of ethnic backgrounds – who are united in their fight against what they see as not only grossly unfair, unjust and dishonest practice but one having intergenerational consequences.

Summing up the Marcellus Protest's influence to date, John thinks that the opposition to fracking has become much more 'respectable' since the summer of 2012 (pers. comm. with the author, 31 January 2013). There is still is not a majority opinion among the general public against shale gas, but the issue has moved from the margins and most people are now aware that fracking is controversial. Before the Protest started, the discovery of shale gas was universally welcomed and those who opposed it were treated as a few 'fanatics' who were easily dismissed. The shale gas industry may yet get its way in Pennsylvania, but it will have to work a lot harder than mere dismissal of its opponents to win its cause. Even if this comes to pass, as a result of community action, it can expect to be heavily regulated.

Anti-fracking in the UK and elsewhere

In Europe, there have been national and EU-wide discussions about how to proceed with shale gas, and opinions are widely spread. Originally, UK regulators and legislators thought that, because the drilling occurs so deep, fracking was unlikely to contaminate groundwater sources and exploration licences were granted to a company called Cuadrilla to sink wells either side of the River Ribble in largely rural parts of coastal Lancashire in England.

During the autumn of 2012, in the political party conference season, the shale gas lobby was very active, calling fringe meetings and trying to build the arguments it thought each party wanted to hear. At the Labour Party fringe (hosted by the Institution of Gas Engineers and Managers), presenters moved from very technical presentations explaining how the walls of the wells are constructed, to emotive pleas to give British people jobs while depriving the greedy gas producers of Qatar of the means to keep themselves furnished with more fast cars. When asked how the industry was prepared to justify an inevitable increase in global warming as a result of the exploitation of unconventional gas sources (IEA, 2012), the spokesmen for shale gas first tried to manoeuvre around the question. He was brought back to the point by an impatient and heckling audience, and then offered the bald riposte 'If you want to avoid global warming, you need to leave the stuff in the ground', leaving a shocked silence in the room.

The aim of this outburst by the spokesman was to bring home the stark expectation (in the gas world) that if we turn off gas, we say goodbye to modern living. However, the effect of the statement was to leave the audience with the clear impression that there was an obvious choice to be made about the kind of energy the UK needed in the future. We could keep burning more fossil fuels, or, if current standards of living were to be preserved, we should leave them in the ground and pursue a less destructive path. But just a week later the Secretary of State for Energy and Climate Change announced that he hoped to press on with fracking. The Chancellor of the Exchequer (the political head of the Treasury) later followed this with a promise of tax breaks to the industry, something his coalition partners were not happy to accept. In the UK, the stage is now set for opposition to shale gas to be played out in the same pattern as in the US. What is interesting is that, in England at least, the motivations for the protesters have been somewhat different.

In early 2011, a calm and placid semi-rural area on the border between north Merseyside and south Lancashire was disturbed by the appearance of an incongruous sight – a drilling rig in the middle of a field. It was one of three test drilling rigs set up by Cuadrilla to see if the underlying Bowland Shale could be as productive as the Marcellus rocks in the USA. Graham, a freelance IT specialist, would not consider himself as an activist of any kind, much less an environmentalist. He had been a member of Greenpeace and Friends of the Earth but never went to a meeting or a protest. But every time he drove past the new drilling site on the outskirts of his village, it bothered him. It just looked wrong, it didn't belong there. And then a few months later Graham's girlfriend went to a meeting at nearby Hesketh Bank village hall. People in the area were gathering, looking for answers as they felt there had been very little notice that exploratory drilling was going to start in their area. At the meeting, the activist group Frack Off explained to everyone how fracking had caused environmental damage in the USA and showed *Gasland*. Many people were upset and worried that this kind of damage could happen on their doorstep, and it was agreed that an organised group, to be called Ribble Estuary Against Fracking or REAF should be formed.

A second meeting a few weeks later attracted 45 people. By this time, talk about fracking was 'viral' across the village and other more organised groups took an interest in the mobilisation to oppose the rig. The UK Green Party, the local Transition Town group and Friends of the Earth all offered to speak and discuss tactics. A few people stepped into a leadership role and the group later settled down into a committed core of about a dozen. Graham, because of his IT experience, had volunteered to set up the group's website and respond to any messages. This was a fairly straightforward duty for a time, but then something associated with the other test well across the estuary happened and the job began to get more demanding.

In the small hours of 1 April 2011, residents of the Fylde peninsula, including the famous Blackpool pleasure beach area, were shaken awake by a minor earthquake measured at magnitude 2.2. The police reported that several people called in expecting pranksters had gone too far in an April fool's joke. However, the next morning revealed that traffic lights had toppled over and there were cracks in pavements and roads and other minor damage.

On 27 May a second earthquake struck in exactly the same place with exactly the same wave profile. This tremor was smaller, measuring magnitude 1.5, but it was enough for regulators to point the finger at the shale gas exploration platform at Preese. A spokesperson for the British Geological Survey said that it was well known that shale gas drilling can cause earthquake activity (Paige, 2011). On 31 May Cuadrilla issued a statement saying it was voluntarily shutting down all of its operations either side of the Ribble until investigations could be completed. The shutdown was likely to last 18 months but on 13 December, just nine months after the earthquake, the government gave permission for the company to resume exploratory operations.

The REAF campaign has always been self-funded and, apart from help from other groups, had no one with campaigning skills when it started. Graham said that early meetings were spent comparing notes with other groups and 'fact sharing'. Their goal, he said, was just to raise awareness and maybe get some things in the papers. They certainly did that, and more. A mass action was organised and a march over 100 strong took place that carried anti-fracking banners through the affected villages. Then REAF started to attract some notable supporters, including Glenda Jackson MP (Labour) and Caroline Lucas MP (Green), and went to Westminster to lobby other Members of

Parliament. The media started to take notice when, early on the morning of 6 August 2011, anti-fracking campaigners climbed 200 metres up the famous Blackpool Tower to display anti-fracking banners. That autumn REAF (mostly Graham) had its hands full fielding approaches by high-profile reporters from programmes like the BBC's *Countryfile*, Bloomberg and Sky News as well as regional TV and radio.

Then, in November, and again in December 2011, Frack Off occupied the Hesketh Bank test rig site. The protesters hung out signs on the rig and shut it down for a number of hours on each occasion. Four people were later found guilty of trespassing and assault charges, despite pointing out that Cuadrilla had flouted the terms of their planning permission and had failed to comply with their own method statement related to the protection of birdlife on the nearby Site of Special Scientific Interest.

Since then, there has been something of a phoney war. The company is not drilling and membership and enthusiasm have dropped off. Attempts to get a wider number of interests involved in the campaign have not been that successful. Local growers who might have been expected to be concerned about surface and groundwater pollution have chosen to keep quiet because they don't want to worry their supermarket customers about the quality of their products.

The lull in hostilities (while the moratorium lasted) gave time for the group to reflect on how their campaign had gone so far. One thing they realised was that they needed clarity about what they wanted next and how they would communicate that to the media. They joined with other activists in the region to re-energise their efforts and it made them think about their tactics and their group organisation to date. They realised that in the early days they did not delegate enough and many enthusiastic people who might have stayed with the group found other things to do away from the campaign. Time and money are a perennial problem for small protest groups, and they worry that when drilling starts up again, they will have problems re-recruiting members.

Graham has also had time to reflect upon his own involvement. He is not convinced that his life is any better now, but he knows that there can be no going back now. The interaction with other environmentalists and local activists has altered his lifestyle. He changed his electricity provider and now buys renewable energy. He grows his own fruit and vegetables and he has learned a lot about leadership and feels he has generally woken up to the world around him.

Just a few kilometres north across the Ribble Estuary, a formidable group of mostly woman had been gathering to oppose the other main drilling site in Lancashire, at Preese Hall Farm near Blackpool. Another rural site, even more remote than the Banks rig, this Cuadrilla operation was proving to be more difficult to fight and Residents Action on Fylde Fracking or RAFF has had to work hard, even after the earthquake, to keep momentum going. The website lists a number of reasons why the group is against fracking including a lack of regulation, potential for air and water pollution, health risks from radioactive sources and chemicals, heavy vehicle traffic, excessive water consumption, the containment of contaminated water for treatment, seismic disturbance and land subsidence, and negative impacts on property prices. Interestingly, the group does not mention greenhouse gas emissions or makes any reference to climate change.

Ann, Pam and Sue are among the most active of the RAFF activists. They say that one official, tired of their repeated and spirited questions and interventions, disparagingly called them the 'hell's grannies'. While meant as an insult, the recounting of this by the woman so called reveals some pride in this label. Ann is retired now but is still very active in the community. She is chair of governors at her local school and volunteers at the library. But she also has some previous experience on pro-environmental issues. Some years earlier she was involved in Save Our Shoreline, a group that lobbied for sewage to be diverted away from the sea and be properly treated. She got involved in anti-fracking after she saw *Gasland* at the library. This was a showing organised by the Co-operative Group, an ethical mutual organisation that traces its roots back to the mid-nineteenth century and is now a multi-billion pound commercial entity active in banking, insurance and many food and non-food retail interests. The Co-op often campaigns on issues that their members suggest and have commissioned reports on the impacts of shale gas and the exploitation of tar sands.

It was about the time of the earthquake that Ann heard that a local group was forming and sought out the meeting place. Pam was also there. Pam (another retiree) had been more active in the environment movement in the past as a member of Greenpeace and as a campaigner against nuclear power, targeting the Sellafield plant located further up the coast north of Blackpool. She became dissatisfied with her Greenpeace membership when that organisation started to focus more on global issues, but had not found a replacement group until she heard about the anti-fracking meeting from her local sand dune officer. The officer was employed to look after the ecologically threatened coastal areas close to where Pam lived. Pam was shocked to hear that the drilling was taking place so close to her home and knew immediately that this was an issue she could get behind.

Sue is an academic and teaches part-time at nearby Lancaster University. Her route to being active in anti-fracking was slightly different. Never tired of learning new things, she had signed up to an Open University course and was doing a module on environmental decision-making. Her assignment required her to find a debate involving the environment and then analyse the decisions that the protagonists made to influence the outcome. When she found out that the earthquake had been caused by fracking, she realised this was an ideal topic for her course. She started reading up on the science and politics of unconventional gas resources and found out where RAFF was meeting. As she become more absorbed in the campaign, she found that her academic detachment was eroding and she became drawn in as a fully active member of the group. RAFF meets in a building in the local park. At first, there were only five people, but they can now boast over 200 on their mailing list and they have been successful in drawing crowds of up to 80 to public meetings. They can be regularly seen on the streets of Blackpool and Lytham St Anne's offering people petitions to sign and handing out leaflets.

Like other anti-fracking groups, the women have been active letter writers and have often contacted the editors of the local newspapers asking them to feature the issue on a regular basis. They have found that the threat to clean water from fracking seems to be the most emotive issue in the area. They live in a coastal area popular with tourists and the amount of water required by the shale gas industry concerns people. When asked about the potentially more damaging effect of greenhouse gas emissions, they find that when they raise this, they are often diverted by people saying that the alternative (renewable energy) is not practical. The opposition to both onshore and off-shore wind farms may explain this hostility. There is a great concern among the RAFF membership that they need to appeal to a broad number of largely conservative-minded people in the area and do not want to appear to be extreme in any way. Earthquakes, traffic congestion and water pollution are all relatively safe ground in Lytham. Windfarms are not. So while they would like to bring in climate change as an additional reason for the opposition to shale gas, they opt to use arguments that will ensure that local support is maintained.

The women say that their tactics are changing now. They have appreciated that they have no foothold in the democratic process, nor do they understand planning procedure as much as they should. They are considering lobbying the Department of Energy and Climate Change (DECC) to impose a proximity rule on the gas industry similar to the one that exists in the United States. This would ensure that no drilling can occur close to housing. They started lobbying their local MP Mark Menzies (Conservative) to ask questions about the industry and the MP responded by helping to set up a shale gas strategy group that includes two government departments and two regulators: the Environment Agency and the Health and Safety Executive. He also was suc-cessful in securing an adjournment debate in Parliament on the regulation of the onshore gas industry on 24 October 2012.

An adjournment debate gives backbench MPs the opportunity to raise issues which the government does not have time to discuss in the Parliamen-tary calendar. The debates are held in the presence of the relevant Minister who is required to respond to the issues that the MPs make. During the debate Mr Menzies called for a number of safeguards for his constituents. He wanted an environmental impact statement to be submitted for every new well and regulations similar to those that govern offshore oil and gas to apply to onshore exploration. He also called for a panel of experts to scrutinise both the exploration and exploitation phases of the shale gas extraction process to ensure that the range of concerns his constituents have expressed are dealt with to (what he termed) a Rolls-Royce standard.

The Minister at the time (John Hayes MP, Conservative) replied to Mr Menzies' concerns by repeating the US shale gas industry's assertions that the methane seepage, as featured in the famous flaming tap scene in *Gasland*, was not associated with deep well fracturing and that (as yet) there was no confirmed evidence of groundwater contamination from the process. He also rejected the claim that the industry uses excessive amounts of water and refuted allegations that fracking causes subsidence. The Minister ended by saying that he would consider further regulations suggested by Mr Menzies but the tenor of his remarks suggested that he felt that the existing safeguards would probably be sufficient to control the industry in the future. His parting shot was that he thought that shale gas represented an exciting opportunity for the country.

In July 2013 George Osborne MP, Chancellor of the Exchequer, announced a generous tax break for shale gas companies, more than halving the amount payable on income from 62 per cent down to 30 per cent (Chestney, 2013). Just a few days later Cuadrilla opened up a new front in the search for UK shale gas reserves by completing the permission process to explore for hydrocarbons near the southern Sussex village of Balcombe. Within days more than 100 protesters were standing in the way of the incoming drilling vehicles. Police made arrests and one truck had its break cable severed. Drilling commenced a few days later but those manning a permanent protest camp on the roadside have promised daily disruption until the company moves off the site.

The geo-politics of this development may influence both the community mobilisation and government support. A survey by Greenpeace (reported in the *Guardian* newspaper) showed that 35 of the 38 MPs who represent constituencies that lie over shale gas deposits in southern England are Conservatives, and many are cabinet ministers in the government (Wintour, 2013). This sets up an interesting conflict of interest which George Osborne (in the same newspaper report) was quick to influence when he said it would be a 'tragedy' if Britain missed out on shale gas exploitation.

This potentially puts the focus back up north where there are fewer constituencies in Coalition hands. But the government was soon to be dismayed to see one of its allies inflaming the recently quiet northern front. Speaking in the House of Lords, the former Energy Minister David (Lord) Howell called for fracking to be concentrated in the north-east of England because it has 'large, desolate and uninhabited areas' (Dominiczak, 2013). Not only did the 'desolate' comment incense people living in north-east, but Howell got the entire region wrong, meaning to say the north-west. After apologising and correcting his mistake, he promptly set off howls of complaint from those already affected in Lancashire.

RAFF and REAF members are not surprised that the Coalition, led by the Conservatives (traditionally a pro-business party), would be anything other than supportive of the oil and gas industry. The stonewall response that their MP received at the time merely confirmed what they suspected; they were on their own. This is sometimes hard to face as RAFF is dealing with continuing challenges like many others fighting fracking across the world. They need to keep members interested, keep money coming in and above all keep the issues fresh in front of the public. Groups like RAFF and REAF will continue to struggle against political and industrial interests that are stacked against them, but this is in the nature of pro-environment struggle and the hell's grannies show no sign of relenting.

It might be tempting to draw a line around the anti-fracking movement as a minority, single-interest pursuit. It would be easy to assume that the groups are populated by the same type of people who will be out next week opposing the latest new road or dam. Some who argue that new gas reserves are vital for the economy might take comfort that there is not a majority lobbying against this form of energy in the way that the consensus in Japan turned against nuclear energy after the Fukushima Daiichi nuclear disaster. A concern for the protesters is that there is evidence that this is correct.

A poll conducted by the University of Texas Austin showed that 63 per cent of a sample of the US public said that they had never heard of or were not familiar with the terms hydraulic fracturing or fracking (UT, 2012). Just 32 per cent said they were familiar with the terms. Of the 752 people who said they were familiar with the terms, just over a third thought that more regulation was needed to control fracking while 22 per cent thought that the industry needed more enforcement of existing laws. A further third thought there was enough or too much regulation. The cognitive gap between gas and climate change was emphasised by two further questions from the survey. When asked if they would vote for a president who supported the expansion of natural gas development, 60 per cent said yes, and yet 65 per cent of the same sample said they thought that global climate change was happening, with 22 per cent claiming it was not.

This will not deter the anti-frackers from their work. Indeed, this is the type of knowledge that makes them re-double their efforts to educate the public to look behind the corporate rhetoric. They share a long and noble tradition of fighting for the preservation of the commons and pointing out that the costs of cleaning up an environmental mess are far more than the costs to prevent it.

The fight against fracking seems to be a genuine coming together of the local and the global. In addition, it plays out beyond environmental impact to political and corporate abuse issues that movements like the Occupy Movement and UK Uncut have brought to the fore in recent times. This could explain the wide appeal the issue has for people of different ages and backgrounds. This heterogeneity of membership has its own intrinsic value such as the ability to respond to different situations or to appeal to new members to join the campaign. But it also means that the groups have access to multiple tactics which makes them more formidable opponents. The way that the fight against fracking has come together could be the template for the next generation of green community groups that want to mount new campaigns for change. But it could also breathe new life into other, much older campaigns that have struggled to maintain public profile and decision-maker support.

4 Green communities in unlikely settings

Big city activism is not always the most fertile ground

Many of the accounts of green community groups in this book and elsewhere focus on people who live in cities. There are many reasons for this. Urban environments are often more tangibly degraded than rural areas, prompting movements for change. Prior to the internet and social networking, the ability to influence others, leading to a collective movement, required numbers to gather to listen to the arguments. This was easier to achieve among denser populations. Once social media took hold, the ability to reach large numbers of people no longer needed a physical presence, and it became far easier to assemble groups to protest at short notice. However, taking action is often more effective when greater numbers congregate for the cause, and this is more likely to happen in larger places. The proximity of individuals to form physical groups has also been important for debate, particularly for those who literally need to see that there is consensus on a point. Others need to debate and work through their own doubts with their peers. People pursuing a variety of causes often still put great store in face-to-face argument and tactical discussion. Finally, decision-makers (a frequent target for campaigners) tend to be found on a regular basis at seats of power, and these are often based in cities.

But it is certainly not the case that pro-environmental activity is only found in towns and cities. Groups such as the Transition Town movement or the charity Global Action Plan have helped to organise groups of people living in smaller-sized locations. Some people who live in more isolated areas seek out one of the many templates, formulas and facilitators available to help them to launch their initiatives. Others start as the result of a galvanising impact such as the threat from a waste facility or a new road and grow from the energy and experience they gain from their campaigns. However, a completely original idea generated from a smaller community happens less frequently.

At about the same time, and just a few miles apart, two very different out-of-the-way communities decided to develop their own brand of green activism. Their efforts developed independent of other influences and focused entirely on the needs and characteristics of their own communities. They did this in settings that, on average, are unusual for the typical green community example. They were both awarded a significant amount of government money for their ideas. The stories behind Ashton Hayes and Blacon show again how very different influences can motivate the instigators of green community groups. They also uphold and support the contention that the diverse and bespoke nature of modern green community action is helping more and more people to make the link between global threats and local action.

'No-go' suburb no more

Ged was working as a Programme Manager for a government scheme called Surestart, which provided services for pre-school children and their families in a town called St Helens near Liverpool. While finding the work rewarding, he decided to follow his interest in environmental improvement work and applied to do a Master's course in Climate Change and Sustainable Development. Ged's dissertation was on the (then) early stages of the Ashton Hayes story, the village in Cheshire that was seeking to be the first to achieve carbon neutrality which is described in more detail later in this chapter.

When Ged took a job with a charity based in the disadvantaged housing estate of Blacon in Chester, he hoped that he might have the opportunity to apply some of the things he learned from his course and his dissertation. This was more in hope than expectation as at the time he took the job there was little scope to do this in a disadvantaged part of a provincial town in England. Blacon was just 15 kilometres from Ashton Hayes, but it might have been on the other side of the planet in terms of the demographics and the history of the community.

Blacon is a neighbourhood that was created from a much smaller settlement after the Second World War to house incoming manual workers required to staff nearby aerospace and steel industries. The post-war building boom produced a dormitory suburb of poorly constructed semi-detached brick housing that was to prove energy-inefficient and increasingly unpopular. Later, in the 1960s and 1970s, a few high-rise housing blocks were added and some middle-income detached housing followed after that. Compared to the highly prized (and highly priced) housing in historic Chester and the surrounding rural county, Blacon represented a rare chance for people with modest incomes to live in the area.

Blacon now houses around 16,000 residents in over 5,200 households and is one of England's largest peripheral estates. Parts of the community (about two-fifths) rank among the top 10 per cent most deprived neighbourhoods in England. But Blacon holds 12 per cent of the City of Chester's population, making it a disproportionate addition to an otherwise affluent tourist town surrounded by prime dairy and arable farmland. The population was (and still is) overwhelmingly white British working class. While the Thatcher administration tried to encourage residents to buy their homes in the 1980s, much of the stock remained in council hands until it was transferred to a third-sector housing association (Chester & District Housing Trust or CDHT) in the year 2000.

While the homogenous nature of the population was not producing multi-cultural friction, Blacon suffered from a lack of investment and an atomisation of service provision where social work, policing, health practitioners and housing professionals all worked to their own agenda, and parts of the area had a reputation for crime and drugs-related problems. The sheer size of the estate made it difficult for community activists to unite the whole area, and pockets of the more disadvantaged parts formed into a close-knit community that considered itself to be on the wrong side of the Chester tracks and proved hard to reach.

This community context was fairly familiar to Ged who had just come from a job in another area that focused on helping marginalised sections of British society. But when he joined the charity in Blacon, there was no sign of things to come. He would be amazed to think that he would become one of the leading lights of a green community movement as the co-ordinator of the popular Sustainable Blacon project.

Ged's original job was to co-ordinate a network of furniture reuse charities across Chester from his base in Blacon. This type of charity work was not remarkable at the time (in 2005) and resembled many around the UK. One of the largest had started in nearby Liverpool. The Furniture Resources Centre (now the FRC Group) later transformed itself from charity to social business by first making their own furniture and then setting up furnished accommodation and logistic businesses hauling recyclates for local government and the private sector.

The Blacon Project set up as a community charity in 1984 and collected old furniture for redistribution to low-income households in the community. The organisation later became the Blacon Community Trust and had a turnover of £1 million in 2010. Today it employs around 40 people and roughly two-thirds of its income is generated by services including childcare, programmes for young people and services and activities for young parents. It also managed a community centre and business advice centre, and still operates the furniture reuse business. In supplying these services, the Trust is following a trend by English local authorities to outsource in an attempt to make diminishing budgets stretch further. Contracting with community businesses and charities (known in other terms as third or non-profit sector organisations) has become fairly widespread in the UK although chronic societal problems do not appear to have improved as a result of this policy.

In 1994, something happened to Blacon that changed it forever. Two newspapers published an article on 'No Go Britain' which featured 50 of the worst places to live in Britain. Blacon was on that list. It was described as an area that suffered drugs and property crime. The article singled out one incident where a police officer was injured when her patrol car was attacked by youths. The area was said to have 15.3 per cent unemployment. This was considerably less than some inner-city wards in nearby Liverpool and Manchester where the ranks of the unemployed in some pockets of those cities were up at around

30 or 40 per cent. Blacon was also much less of a concern to the government than some of the other notorious outposts on the list. Estates in provincial towns like Plymouth in the south-west and Stockton in the north-east had to cope with joblessness that affected almost half of the working population in the early 1990s. Blacon certainly had its problems, but probably attracted attention because, being surrounded by much more affluent areas, it stuck out as a place of notoriety and complaint.

The articles upset Blacon's residents and both local and national political representatives. Gyles Brandreth, the MP for Chester at the time, raised the issue in Parliament, calling for a debate on the scandalous treatment of his constituents by the press. He complained that *The Independent on Sunday* and the *Daily Mirror* had printed 'a travesty of the truth and an insult to the good people of Blacon, who meet challenges with good humour, resilience and the will to overcome them'. He went on to say that 'a fine community has been traduced by two national newspapers' and asked the Leader of the House if he could have a debate 'to explore how newspapers can slander such communities without any justification' (Hansard, 1994).

The articles led to a series of meetings and events to show the rest of the country that Blacon was not a 'no-go' area. Activities included a late night walk by local people, including several pensioners, to demonstrate that the neighbourhood was safe. This show of solidarity was led by the politicians who took advantage of the sympathy that the articles attracted to lobby for more resources for Blacon. There was only limited success for this until the incoming Labour administration in 1997 reviewed the way communities were being supported. Later, Labour introduced a new national integrated neighbourhood management programme and in 2001 Blacon was one of the first areas to benefit from this. The programme required intervening agencies to work together and to include the community in a range of decisions from budget spending to strategy. While there was not much on environmental improvement, the sub-programmes on housing improvement, better green space and 'image and infrastructure' gave local people and community workers the chance to influence local plans. This consequently gave scope to access resources for good ideas that fell under the designated themes.

A 'One Voice for Blacon' group was set up to co-ordinate community initiatives. In 2006, Ged joined the 'Image and Infrastructure' group, representing the Trust and became its co-ordinator in 2007. Meanwhile, the Trust saw that sustainability was going to feature in the area's Vision and Action Plan and formed a group of advisers to help with bids and lobby for change with its partners. Consequently, a feasibility study was produced by the Trust which would become the basis of a sustainable energy blueprint for the estate. This included biofuel boilers for high-rise flats, wind turbines and an ambitious programme for a renewable energy-powered business park. There was also energy retrofit work planned for the existing housing stock.

The first project to be implemented under the new strategy was the improvement of a green space. Led by a local man and one of the Trust's volunteer advisers, the plan was to create a community focal point around the cycle path built along a former railway track. The old Blacon Station site became the centre of attention and a rallying point for those who wanted to convince more people in the community that their environment was worth fighting for. The line had been closed for decades, leaving a derelict building that had been a magnet for youths and the site of anti-social behaviour. The Trust attracted other funding partners including the council, CDHT and the National Lottery to transform the area with new fencing, signs and benches, all with a railway theme. Five schools made over 1,000 tiles to form a colourful mosaic centrepiece for the scheme and this built ownership among young people in the area. The site continues to be maintained by the council and the community transport organisation Sustrans. Volunteers clean the area every day and remain on the site to offer a welcome to walkers and cyclists who are passing through.

Finally completed in 2010, the Old Station project received widespread recognition, but it was the community involvement that this small scheme generated that encouraged Ged to find more projects for the Trust to promote. In July 2009, Sustainable Blacon was formed, with its Board comprised of local residents, agency stakeholders (the council and CDHT) and expert advisers on energy, green spaces and urban design. Just six months later the new organisation was the successful recipient of almost £400,000 of Department of Energy and Climate Change (DECC) grant money for a green community project. Called the Low Carbon Communities Challenge (LCCC), Blacon was one of 22 UK communities to benefit from the programme which aimed to find ways to reduce energy-related impacts on the environment. In Blacon this meant trying to make a 20 per cent reduction in domestic energy consumption through community education and demonstration.

The award was crucial to Ged and the fledgling Sustainable Blacon concept because up until that point there was simply not enough money to implement the feasibility plan that accompanied the new initiative. Before the DECC money, there had been a failed attempt to get funding from a range of sources. This led Ged to understand that his initial ideas were not big enough to interest funders. The policy consensus at the time was that the problem of climate change was so large that only grand statements and programmes that would involve hundreds or thousands of households would be sufficient to merit government support.

The money from the DECC was used to fund a programme in Blacon that was split into two distinct strands. The first sought to establish two demonstration homes which would be equipped with low-energy appliances and technologies. But the programme recognised that energy was not an issue for everyone and so it also featured other sustainable living initiatives such as waste and recycling, water conservation, sustainable transport (cycling, walking and public transport) and growing fruit and vegetables. The whole programme was designed to show Blacon residents that sustainable living can work in practice rather than try to get the message across though presentations or leaflets. The show homes were staffed by people from the community who were trained to give advice and were able to direct interested residents to government-sponsored assistance. Their involvement was crucial as it was reasoned that they were the best messengers because they were trusted local people and not professionals.

The second strand would create a 12-month experiment to discover the best way to motivate residents to reduce their greenhouse gas emissions. A group of 150 households, drawn from the community and in particular from Blacon's many community and faith groups, were offered an eight-session community education programme. This included free advice and support to focus on energy, carbon, waste, food and water. The group was sub-divided into three. The first group were given instruction but had no additional energy measures fitted in their houses. The second group had their energy consumption monitored and were given access to this data. The third group had internet-based energy management equipment fitted in their houses.

The data set was so enticing that six universities lined up to ask to help with the measurement and analysis of results and to study the impacts. Ged thought it was important to show participants that there was widespread approval of what they were trying to achieve in a community not normally used to praise and encouragement. He pinned one quote from the then Energy and Climate Change Minister, Joan Ruddock MP, to one of the showhouse walls to show them that important people were taking notice of their actions. The quote read: 'There's a real appetite out there to save energy to help tackle global warming and save money on fuel bills. Blacon will help to develop the policies we need in the future to make the successful transition to a low carbon economy.' Ed Miliband (now leader of the Labour Party) was Secretary of State at the Department for Energy and Climate Change at the time and came to visit the project as more and more people became interested in the sustainable design and community work in Blacon.

When the official evaluation report of the Low Carbon Community Challenge was published, it said that 'there is little evidence of widespread change in attitudes, behaviours or the take up of low carbon measures' (DECC, 2012b). This might have disappointed readers if they had stopped there, but a thorough examination of the document revealed the full value of the programme. The report went on to say: 'While financial savings were an important initial hook to engage their local communities (i.e. extrinsic motivations), once involved, people were motivated more by a sense of community and social interaction (i.e. intrinsic motivations).' This is the same finding that was made in the report on the Britain in Bloom programme (RHS, 2011).

The report also said that 'visible measures sparked interest and instilled confidence with some households' and confirmed the understanding from other projects that people are influenced by those around them. The report documented the finding that people with very little disposable income were still willing to explore new technology such as solar (photovoltaic) electricity after seeing neighbours, or 'people like them', installing them on their houses.

Again, this reinforces work elsewhere, in this case the experiments that Schultz *et al.* (2007) carried out on residents' justification for buying energy-saving products in California. The finding of the LCCC evaluation was that people said it was important that 'trusted local advisors' or 'go-to' local residents were able to speak to neighbours who might not have paid the same attention to a representative of an energy company or the local authority. Ged said that there was also evidence in Blacon and other participating communities that feelings of belonging and commitment had strengthened as a result of the activities within the project.

Almost four years on, Ged admits that there have been no iconic achievements that he can point to as a result of the efforts of Sustainable Blacon. However, he knows that it has had a lasting effect on many community members who would not have considered the impact they were having on the environment without the programme. Anecdotal evidence suggests that many people have been inspired and the general perception is that Blacon is a more sustainable place. Many know that the 'no-go' label has been relegated to history as a result of the positive press that the community has received over the period that the programme has run.

Over half (= 92) of the 170 households that were recruited completed the energy education programme. While there was only a small average reduction in the energy consumption of the households, there was a wide variation within that group, pointing to a sub-set of residents who made very large savings. There was a core of committed residents who attended eight meetings and were taken on a trip to an exemplar project at the Centre for Alternative Technology in Wales. Planning meetings and group discussions regularly attracted well over 100 people at the height of the activities.

Now, as the DECC money has come to an end, the number of activists is down to a committed dozen. But these activists are still coming up with new ideas and practical actions all the time. From January to April 2012 the team developed a Save Money Keep Warm (SMKW) project where groups of vulnerable older people and young children from across west Cheshire visited the Blacon Eco House. The team followed this up with a Home Energy Assessment which helped to fit basic energy- and water-saving measures and referred residents to other agencies for help where appropriate. The government and the water conservation NGO Waterwise recognised this cumulative effort with an award in the 'community-led initiative' category. The SMKW was so successful that project was continued for a second year, this time helping people to switch energy tariffs and clear winter snow.

Ged left the Sustainable Blacon programme in 2012 to take up a new job with CAFOD, the Catholic anti-poverty charity which focuses on the developing world. CAFOD is a member of the charity coalition Stop Climate Chaos and Ged has pledged that the lessons he learned from his time in Blacon will be carried over into his new assignment where the impacts of climate change are experienced in much starker terms. Some of these lessons included the importance of the personal approach. He now knows that one-to-one meetings are far more effective than impersonal information that is often handed out on paper or distributed online. The motivation to save money is still the primary reason for people taking a first interest in energy conservation. However, when he talked to people in more depth, he found that there was a considerable concern and awareness of the potential dangers of climate change. People were just not that confident about expressing or acting on their worries.

He also found that while people were interested in hearing about the technical and practical specifics of the energy and climate change programme, they were more interested in getting out of their houses and meeting each other to talk it over with their peers. This is a common theme that occurs again and again when people are asked to talk about green community initiatives. It seems that the isolation that many feel, coupled with the concern about deteriorating environmental conditions, produces a readymade audience for communal participation in green issues.

This is a good start, but it is not enough to keep people interested over the longer term. As Ged found out at Blacon, when the money runs out and the media lights turn to the next new idea, it gets harder to retain the interest of many participants. But he and others would argue that the retention of a core group of energised people is often the real prize for short-term projects. In areas where there is no cohesive starting point or existing organisation, the outputs of this type of project are numbers trained or houses treated, but the outcome is a residual group that will continue to try to influence their community long after the limelight and the money have disappeared.

Finally, there was a balance that Ged tried to strike between community empowerment and collaboration. This is also something that others like the Transition Town movement have considered. For these places, self-sufficiency and self-reliance are the key to sustainable survival. Transition Towns believe that a reliance on authorities or corporations can lead to a compromise of interests when resources diminish. Ged started out with these ideals too. But while the achievements of Sustainable Blacon are all the more powerful for the fact that they were conceived and staffed by local people, he accepts that it might have been more fruitful to accept more help from the council and other local housing bodies. Access to funding was one area that he thinks would have improved if he had cultivated more powerful friends.

Ultimately, the economic slow-down has meant that funding for this sort of work has all but dried up. The only option in order to maintain a regular staff team would have been to sell Sustainable Blacon's expertise as a service in some form. In a disadvantaged community and with public funding in decline, this is well nigh impossible. At the same time, the LCCC programme absorbed so much of Sustainable Blacon's time and energy that it was unable to develop further projects. Ged and others prepared a business plan for a Recycle Your Cycle project and they demonstrated that it could be a success if there was start-up funding available. They also helped bring the local bus companies together, leading to improved services. However, keeping up the numbers of local volunteers involved in planning, and improving and maintaining green spaces, has been a challenge. But these are all things that have made Ged stronger and there is very little regret when he recounts the Sustainable Blacon story. He takes satisfaction in the knowledge that good things happened in a former 'no-go' community.

Big things can happen in small places

Garry did an environmental science degree before starting work as a hydrologist. After two years he embarked on a new career in journalism after a Master's degree in Public Health Engineering. Fitting in a few extended stays in Africa and the Middle East along the way, he co-founded Technical Editing Services with his wife Anne in 1988 and based himself in Ashton Hayes, where he has lived for 30 years. He sold his business to the environmental consultancy RSK Group in 2007 and now sits on its Board. Garry says that he always tried to live and work in a sustainable manner (at least as much as his business would allow), but that was the extent of his ambitions until he visited the Hay Festival. The festival takes place in the small village of Hay-on-Wye in Herefordshire on the Welsh border. The festival now attracts 50,000 visitors who listen to talks by world-famous authors. Hay is a haven for book buyers and literary merchandise and showcases its status with the annual festival that mainly concentrates on arts and literature.

Garry went along to hear a discussion led by Sir David King, then chief scientist to the UK government. He was joined on the platform by the then Chairman of Shell, Lord Oxburgh. They were talking about climate change so it promised to be a worthwhile session. King summarised the dire predictions that climate scientists were making then (and now) and talked about government and industry actions to mitigate the effects before issuing a challenge to the 1,500-strong audience. His message was that change starts with your own actions. He asked the audience to think about what they could do – 'we are all in this together' was the theme.

Garry left the debate and started to think that, while Oxburgh was trying to influence large company behaviour, a village like his could probably respond in a similar way if enough residents decided to act together. This was the summer of 2005 and that session in Hay-on-Wye turned out to be the inspiration that encouraged Garry to take actions that would affect his life and the lives of many others for the foreseeable future.

Ashton Hayes is a small settlement in North Cheshire about eight miles from the market town of Chester. It lies on the Cheshire plain, a fertile farming area famous for its dairy herds. Milk farmers have struggled in the UK in recent years as supermarkets discount staple foods, driving milk prices down as a result. Consequently, four of the six farms around the village have folded in the past 20 years and some of the other agricultural buildings now house more modern businesses like PR agencies and financial advisors. Many residents choose to live in the pleasant surroundings of the village but travel to work in the nearby cities of Liverpool and Manchester. Ashton Hayes now has a population of around 1,000 people living in about 410 homes. When people move to the village, they tend to stay, making for a very stable community. There is a good social fabric but it's not remarkable in that sense compared to others in the area.

A few months after his visit to Hay, Garry was meeting friends at the village pub quiz when he started a conversation based on what he had heard at the festival. He wondered if it would be possible to get the support of the other villagers to make a special effort to reduce their environmental impact. His good friend, Roy 'Alex' Alexander, the Professor of Environmental Sustainability at the local University of Chester, enthusiastically backed the idea and this gave Garry the confidence to embark on a number of discussions with others that might be supportive of the radical idea that was forming in his head.

Finally, he was ready and asked if he could address the parish council in November 2005 as a concerned citizen. Garry spoke for ten minutes. He explained his concern about the effects of global warming and reminded the councillors of the changes happening in the countryside surrounding the village. He said that while many people were taking action in nearby cities, such as Manchester, and in some companies, no single village had declared its intention to go carbon neutral. He related this to the councillors' responsibilities to reduce the village's impacts on the environment so that the generation represented by their grandchildren would look back on their actions and respect them for trying to leave the community as they found it. But he also talked about the responsibility of preparing the villagers to cope with future changes.

He tried to make it as easy as possible for the councillors to agree by saying that the project – to create England's first carbon neutral village – would never touch a penny of the parish council funds. Alex also said the University of Chester could send students to do the annual leg-work needed to obtain information about the villagers' energy habits. Garry committed to running the project for five years and agreed to take up the vacant seat on the council. Garry warned that the press would be interested but offered to handle that as well, and then read out an impressive list of those who had already pledged to help, including the government-backed Energy Saving Trust and a number of influential residents who were willing to donate some land to a tree-planting initiative.

The council voted narrowly three to two to support Garry's suggestions, but there were a number of conditions, in addition to joining the council. They also asked Garry to hold a public meeting to demonstrate that there was enough community support to back the idea and that any learning would be shared with the world at large. Now that the project was 'real' and had the parish council behind it, Garry got together with Alex. They decided that the carbon neutral project should involve everyone, but they would not compel anyone to join in if they decided they were not interested. They also agreed never to argue with anyone about climate change or accept political speeches at meetings. They appreciated that many of the villagers would not immediately understand why the council had agreed to their plan and so the title for the project 'Aiming to Become Carbon Neutral' tried to convey a journey rather than a foregone conclusion – something they could not guarantee, in any case.

The initiative badly needed funds to get started. Garry phoned local businesses for money and raised more than £3,600 in just a few days. He used the money to create road signs saying 'Ashton Hayes – Aiming to become England's first carbon neutral village' and advertised the initiative on a new website: www.goingcarbonneutral.co.uk. The signs appeared on railings and under the official roadside place sign so that motorists would be under no doubt about the aspirations of this small rural settlement. No permission was sought or given for this new signage. The next step was to get some publicity and Garry got articles in the local paper that talked about environmental issues.

The website boldly stated that the initiative was committed to helping 'everyone in their community to think about how their way of life affects their impact on climate change and to help people to understand how simple actions can make a big impact on CO_2 emissions to the atmosphere'. From this modest outlet the story began to catch the eye of wider media reporters. The BBC's regional news programme *Northwest Tonight* asked to come to the village to film and Garry took advantage of this by asking if the BBC would interview local primary schoolchildren at the front of their display of 'vehicles of the future'. This caused a buzz throughout the village as it was rare for Ashton Hayes to be featured on television.

The official project launch took place on 26 January 2006. It was a freezing night, but almost 75 per cent of the whole village (adults) squeezed into the school hall. The Women's Institute offered apple pie and the project used donated cash to buy 'English champagne' as refreshments. A range of people were lined up to speak but none was given more than ten minutes. If people spoke for longer than that, they were physically removed, in an amusing way, which caused much merriment among the audience. The people who spoke asked the audience if they thought they could change their lifestyles and offered all kinds of ways to help. The turn-out and the coverage settled the parish councillors' minds about support and the campaign was off and running. To everyone's surprise, the BBC World Service radio came along and broadcast the event to 12 million listeners.

In the following weeks and months efforts were stepped up to show that the momentum was growing. In May that year, Alex organised some of his students to come to the village to do a baseline survey of people's attitudes and energy habits, so they could measure the effect of their efforts at a later date. After a year the effect was confirmed as there had been a 20 per cent drop in energy consumed by the village as measured by home energy bills and travel and transport habits. Many of these early achievements were due to the acquisition of low-energy products such as compact fluorescent light bulbs, the adoption of good habits such as turning things off, and better energy management at home. People were encouraged to change behaviour first before considering spending their money on renewable energy technology.

More press and TV from around the world started to take interest. The villagers liked the attention and Garry's journalistic experience was useful in responding to calls for interviews and organising photo opportunities. He also trained local people in interview techniques. They realised from the launch meeting that people enjoyed coming together and organised more meetings where they showed their home-produced films or laid on talks about how to save energy in the home or install and use renewable energy.

As more people in the village started to take an interest in the initiative, Garry and Alex formed specialist groups and then realised that they needed to establish some ground rules that concentrated on avoiding the alienation of any section of the village. They redoubled their efforts never to argue with people who refused to take part. They also agreed and tried hard not to allow politicians to take any credit for the project, including banning them from speaking at any of their public meetings. All parties (including their own Member of Parliament) were still invited to attend meetings, but they had to sit quietly in the audience and listen. It was not a popular decision with the politicians, particularly when they could see there were TV cameras in the room, but it ensured that nobody was put off by associating what they were doing with political party policies or personalities.

The survey work showed that most people were interested in saving money and energy. The original motivation for the project was loftier – to protect future generations – but Garry and Alex reasoned that any means that drew people to take an interest in what they were trying to do would be acceptable. They were very serious about how they thought their generation would be regarded by their grandchildren and they continually asked themselves what future generations would think of how they and their peers treated the environment. This legacy of thinking continues to be one of the prime movers for all their actions.

The next challenge was to try to spread the ownership of the scheme. The growing media interest meant that the project team and residents were continually in front of microphones and cameras. They started asking other villagers if they were prepared to tell their stories to reporters and then they made sure that they didn't put up the same people all the time. A major breakthrough came when Barry Cooney became an overnight sensation. Barry ran the local pub and initially argued against the initiative, saying it was a waste of time. But when Barry was faced with big energy bills, he asked the team if they could do an energy audit at the pub and suggest ways that he could pay less for his electricity and gas.

They noticed that Barry ran the chillers for his beers and other drinks on a 24-hour basis, even in winter. A simple timer helped him to save over £200. There were other recommendations. The auditor pointed out that it was not necessary to turn the ovens on until they were ready to be used and that the cigarette machine did not need to be on all night. Not only was Barry better off, but the brewery was also delighted with the media coverage. Barry appeared in a film made by Inigo Gilmour for the Live Earth 2007 rock concert called *The Village Greened*, which was first shown at Wembley Stadium in London. The film was seen worldwide and many publicans started to call Barry for advice. He became an advocate for energy savings in pubs and clubs and the Deuchars brewery later invited him to Scotland where they presented him with an award and a free holiday.

Now there was real momentum behind the Ashton Hayes Going Carbon Neutral bandwagon and the organising committee realised that it needed some serious money to make a bigger difference. They started looking for grants from government and were successful with a few small grants from the Environment Ministry (DEFRA) and others. But the big breakthrough came from the same source that helped Sustainable Blacon to take off: the Low Carbon Community Challenge or LCCC. The cheque from the Department of Energy and Climate Change (DECC) gave Ashton Hayes over £410,000 to spend on projects to install renewable energy, including solar electric and micro-grid projects.

Some of the issues that were associated with these projects required some lengthy and complicated advice about ownership, liability and legal rights. Instead of spending large amounts of their grant money on costly advice, Garry and others help to set up the Carbon Leapfrog Charity in London. This recruited professionals to offer pro bono professional advice to community groups that wanted to emulate the Ashton Hayes example. There are now over 50 towns and villages that have been inspired by the example of Ashton Hayes and many are using the Carbon Leapfrog service.

Garry reflects that after seven years of hard but enjoyable work, a number of lessons have been learned. He has come to see that there is a need to keep on raising awareness and showing progress, even in a community that is so committed to the idea of mitigating climate change. Being inclusive while not being aggressive was found to be the best policy in a small village environment. Meeting regularly in comfortable and interesting places with lots of food and drink worked well to keep the curious but not yet committed coming to gatherings. The meetings needed to be useful and informative, but earnestness was to be avoided. These were serious issues they were dealing with, but they combined a sense of fun with their initiatives whenever this was possible.

Measuring and communicating progress were relatively easy with the connections Alex had made through the university. But it was still important to convey this in a manner that would encourage the villagers to keep on improving. The website carries a running set of statistics stretching back to 2006 when measurements began. Much of it makes impressive reading. To date, the entire village has reduced its domestic carbon emissions by 23 per cent.

Almost every villager now recycles their rubbish and uses low-energy light bulbs which is perhaps expected in a country that has made it easy for consumers to make these changes. But in 2006 only around 35 per cent set their washing machines to wash at low temperatures (30°C). By 2010, that figure had grown to more than 70 per cent. The surveys went beyond household energy, showing that just over 30 per cent bought local produce at the start, rising to over 80 per cent at the most recent count. There is also some interesting detail in the Ashton Hayes surveys. In a comparison of 59 similar households, there was a limited but progressive reduction in home energy-consumption. But over the same period the travel patterns were less predictable. While there has been virtually no change in car use, villagers reduced their airtravel by over one third. Clearly more detailed investigation would be needed to tease out the attribution for this behaviour changeas it might be that those households were affected by the economic downturn, for example. However, the comparative information is invaluable as studies show that people are significantly affected by their perception of how others around them behave (Schultz *et al.*, 2007).

By 2012, the village had obtained and installed an impressive range of low-carbon technology, including a Nissan Leaf electric pool car, a carbon neutral sports pavilion and a solar roof for the local school. As the project matured, they found that some adjustments were necessary. After the first years of achievements were bedded in and the flood of media interest subsided, the team decided to deflect new media requests for interviews to other worthwhile projects. Another issue that has arisen is the inevitable slow-down of the amount of energy that has been saved. This is typical of many projects that are at first taken up with the harvesting of lower-hanging fruit and then find the next wave is a little harder to achieve.

But this is a project that is seeking carbon neutrality and they are constantly looking for new ways to drive down energy consumption and install more renewable energy generation. There are strong positives from the Ashton Hayes story thus far, not least because it might have been the case that early energy-saving gains were followed by complacency or rebound behaviour (using more energy as a reward for good behaviour), but this seems to have been avoided by the villagers.

To keep the momentum going, they have renewed interest in behaviour change beyond the technical interventions. They realise that in psychological terms work in this area is completely different from trying to get residents to accept the introduction of physical interventions in their houses. Habitual behaviour change requires a sense that lives as they have been lived to date are no longer appropriate in a changing world. The effort to do this goes well beyond influencing an occasional consumer decision. In Ashton Hayes both approaches have been followed from the outset with a strong emphasis on longer-term behavioural change backed up by annual surveys and bespoke feedback to individual households by Alex and his University of Chester team. However, there is a feeling that, with grants harder to come by in a recession, long-term behaviour change may move the village towards its target at a faster pace.

Consequently the Going Carbon Neutral committee has become more interested in individuals coming forward to ask for help to change their own behaviour. Not only does this represent a way to further drive down energy consumption, but it can sometimes help to recruit others who have been slower to participate in the initiative. Richard, an electrical engineer, asked if he could experiment with smart meters and came back with a handful of spreadsheets which showed the energy he was able to save through better management of his appliances. The group then publicised his success and soon he was being invited to other people's houses. The move was more effective than a power company employee or consultant doing the same job because everyone knew Richard. They trusted him to give them the right advice. This and the visual demonstration offered by the meter was an effective tool in changing wasteful behaviour such as leaving electrical equipment on standby and leaving appliances switched on at the wall socket.

In more reflective moments Garry and Alex point out that they don't feel they have hit a wall because they know that the culture of the village has been permanently changed. The parish council is developing a neighbourhood plan that will seek to embed energy-saving habits, and the regular round of surveys reminds residents that the carbon neutral programme is still going. The annual visits by the survey team also prompt them to keep energy consumption in mind at all times.

They say that the lower profile in terms of media coverage may make it appear that the world is losing interest in their project, but it was a conscious decision to divert coverage away from the village. Whereas previously the coverage helped some sceptics in the village to support the project, continuing coverage has proven to be more of a distraction than a help. Like other groups that have attracted world interest for what they have achieved, they are proud to have inspired green community activity in other places. But this can be a double-edged sword as it also saps the strength from their efforts to achieve new things in the village. There was a time when many of them were spending more time away from the village at speaking engagements than they were working on their own project.

The Going Carbon Neutral programme has touched more than two-thirds of the village (72 per cent of all householders have completed at least one survey) and after the first six years 120 households are still active in one way or another. Like Ged, they found that it was the personal touch that made the difference, such as door-to-door surveys rather than mailing out questionnaires. They appreciate that there will be a percentage who may never be interested in participating in their activities but they are still interested in this section of the village. When asked why people have not engaged with what they are doing, very few said that they were in outright opposition to the idea of a low-carbon village. Indeed, many said that they were concerned about energy conservation but did not feel they wanted to join in with a group project.

There are many explanations for this including the reverse effect of positive norm-based influencing – the concern that an individual's efforts will reveal that they are inferior to their neighbours. People who are worried about this tend to avoid revealing details about the way they live and consume energy in case they compare poorly to others. These people could very well be out-performing other households in energy conservation, but the fear of failure or scrutiny keeps them from joining in. Others may feel that the issue of mitigating climate change is too much for one family or even one village and that the government should be leading the way. To reach these pockets of people requires the employment of different tactics which is why Ashton Hayes has started asking more searching questions about influencing and behaviour change.

They have looked at the ways that other villages have been running their sustainability programmes. In Bollington on the other side of the county, they saw that a lot of time had been spent gathering statistics about existing and expected performance before they chose their course of action. In Ashton Hayes they decided that while this was prudent, they were impatient to get started and followed a more action-orientated approach. Later they realised that the visible signs that things were happening were also important. The committee has now committed to creating some form of action (a meeting, a press announcement, an excursion or a grand opening) in Ashton Hayes every three months, regardless of its relative impact or if it had been written into the original action plan.

They tried to get the sub-groups engaged in specific projects rather than having smaller groups of people managing individual projects. The groups ranged from those interested in the micro-grid project or the school curriculum through to communication and tree-planting. A programme meeting was held every six to eight weeks to co-ordinate their efforts. Each project was constantly assessed to make sure it did not present an open-ended commitment. This avoided wasting time and energy on ideas that were unlikely to be completed. All sub-group members were volunteers so it was important that everybody always felt they were doing the job that played to their strengths.

To recruit new project members they often employed the 'people like me' tactic. If they thought that there was a resident with certain skills or interests, they asked someone of a similar age to approach the prospective member of the group first. They also noticed that people seemed to be more enthusiastic about doing something in their own homes when they had the advantage of seeing what happened in other people's homes. One couple who had offered support to Garry right from the start had converted their impressive home into a low-carbon house. After seeking permission Garry and Alex capitalised on this by holding meetings there. Not only did this help to demonstrate some of the energy-saving measures that they were hoping others would adopt, but it satisfied a deep curiosity by many to have a good look inside a house that they had walked past on countless occasions.

After a while it was decided to map the skills of the active groups which, after the first two years, comprised of around 20 different people. Around 15 regularly attended the planning meetings. During the review the working parties on new technology, new ways to advise residents through ideas like a 'carbon clinic', and a carbon sink group thinking about new areas for tree planting were reconfigured. In addition, a conference and communications team was set up to make sure the right amount of effort was expended on disseminating their ideas to other communities. Over this period some left the group due to the pressure of their day jobs or because of the amount of work they needed to do to keep the group going. But these cases were very rare and most of the people who responded to Garry and Alex at the very start are still working for the cause.

The school programme was particularly successful. They had worked hard to engage the children and their teachers who collected information about various aspects of the energy-saving efforts in the village for projects and displays. The headmaster was supportive and was happy to invite the Energy Saving Trust's education officer to visit the school to help the children understand how energy is generated and energy conservation. The children also mapped the trees in the village and science projects experimented on the smart meters that were given to the school by donors. There was even a Year 6 competition which focused on cars of the future.

Because of all this activity, parents readily agreed for their kids to be filmed by news crews and to appear in the shorts that were made for the Going Carbon Neutral website. This could have been a difficult area as many parents are aware of child protection issues and some could have been wary about allowing their children to be featured in the media. However, with parental support the children were an integral part of the initiative, showing that the intergenerational aspect of the project was more than just fine words.

Bringing other organisations into the village was also helpful. Oxfam contacted the village and asked if the school would like to participate in a project that matched people living in developing countries that were under the threats caused by global warming with those working to limit these impacts in the UK. As a result, Oxfam brought women from a Bangladeshi river island community to the village. The high point was a session at the school when the children asked the women what kind of lives they led and how they were threatened by flooding caused by climate change.

In another international link, the village's achievements were discovered by a Norwegian community south of Oslo, called Notteroy. Their representative got in touch with the Going Carbon Neutral committee and invited them over so they could show how Ashton Hayes had inspired their own efforts to respond to the challenge of climate change. Garry and a few others were very happy to accept the Norwegian community's offer.

Even now, the will to keep the momentum going is in the forefront of Garry and Alex's minds. It is hard to step away from a commitment to go carbon neutral before you achieve neutrality. They appreciate that the grants are time-limited and that they have to have a more economically sustainable model in order to continue with the initiative. New building projects in the village have been rare but influential – the new energy-efficient sports hall being the most notable. They are also considering how new developments could be heated by a district combined heat and power unit. These projects give the opportunity to show off new technology to both the rest of the village and the outside world. But the treatment of existing buildings (where most people live) has led to a bigger contribution to lowering the energy consumption of the village. They also have their eye on some under-used or disused structures and have plans to rationalise and convert some of these into low-energy businesses or homes.

The latest idea is to create an energy company. Over time there has been a considerable amount of renewable energy and smart grid technology installed across the village following the successful application for numerous grants and donations from industry. Some communities have sought to connect their sustainable energy generation together through a commonly owned Energy Service Company or ESCO. The thinking at Ashton Hayes is that if their total output could be managed and co-ordinated through one central point, as opposed to independent building-by-building systems, then it might be made to work more efficiently. To this end a Community Interest Company will act as the village energy manager, pooling all the assets that they have built up over the past five years.

Another proposal aimed at generating new funding is to issue a share offer. This could promise a return on investment in the village energy company as the sale of renewable energy into the national grid starts to generate profits. This could be turned into annual yields for investors. There have also been more traditional ideas to generate income including their plan to buy the local store and run it as a successful community shop, staffed mainly by volunteers.

When you stand back and consider the entirety of the things that Garry and Alex and the rest of the Ashton Hayes villagers have achieved, it can seem a little daunting. This is not necessarily because of the ambition of their projects or the energy that they have saved, although this has been impressive. They would be the first to admit that many other places have managed to install similar types of technology, plant trees and involve school children in pro-environment projects. But not many of these projects hang the immense responsibility of generational accountability on their actions. More than many similar projects, the Ashton Hayes work clings tightly to that aspect of the 'Bruntland definition' of sustainability: to live in a way that meets the needs of current generations without compromising the ability of future generations to meet their own needs. Or perhaps more appropriately they are following the old Native American proverb that we do not inherit the Earth from our ancestors, we borrow it from our children.

Some may say that this all sounds impossibly laudable and a motive that others are unlikely to share. But in an interview on national breakfast television, Prince Charles, following the announcement that his son William's wife Kate was pregnant, said:

> I've gone on for years about the importance of thinking about the long term in relation to the environmental damage, climate change and

everything else. We don't, in a sensible world, want to hand on an increasingly dysfunctional world to our grandchildren, to leave them with the real problem. I don't want to be confronted by my future grandchild and (have) them say: 'Why didn't you do something?' So clearly now that we will have a grandchild, it makes it even more obvious to try and make sure we leave them something that isn't a total poisoned chalice.

(ITV, 2013)

The Prince has indeed gone on record many times to talk about the dangers of climate change and other environmental impacts. Support from royalty helps the cause of the green community activist, but many more people are becoming convinced to take action because of the convictions of ordinary people living around them. As we have seen, many green community initiatives are sparked and led by people who are acutely affected by feelings of injustice and moral outrage about what is happening to the world. Garry's speech to the parish council explicitly pointed out the inter-generational aspect of the project and consequently it has been knitted into the mission of the village. Sometimes they feel it is hard to live up to their reputation as environmental fixers and the fathers of the village vision. But it is not hard to imagine that in weaker moments they only have to look their grandchildren in the eye before redoubling their efforts. This may seem to some like an intolerable self-inflicted pressure that they have put themselves under, and yet it is hard to think of a more effective spur to action.

5   From Timperley to Larimer
Two journeys of inspiration

Introduction

There are many examples over the past half-century where communities have organised to confront a real or perceived threat to their area or to improve and enhance what they already have. But this is certainly not a universal situation and there are many more places that, for one reason or another, are at risk or suffer degraded environments that they have not or cannot organise to affect change. This chapter looks at two communities that historically have not organised for their environment, but have recently started to challenge and change the forces that affect them in very different ways.

Both communities have benefited from inspirational leaders who have very different stories and have approached the obstacles in their path in very different ways. Later we will consider the progress of the neighbourhood of Larimer, an underinvested African-American area in the US city of Pittsburgh. This is an example of how environmental issues grew, not from a sense of environmental protection, but from an extension of the fight for social justice.

Learning to live with climate change: community awakening in south-west Manchester

The first story describes the transformation of a quiet suburb of a city in north-west England: Manchester. Occasionally communities respond to influences not from within, but from without. Timperley, on the western urban fringe of the Manchester conurbation, did not have an organised resident association and only managed sporadic and sparse attendance when meetings were called about the threat to their community from flooding. The influences of a research project from a nearby university and a peripatetic green community group changed that and now the community convenes an active green community group.

The name of the original town of Timperley is derived from 'Timber Leah', the Anglo-Saxon term for a clearing in a wood. Like many suburbs of expanding industrial cities, Timperley started as a small feudal settlement. Over the centuries it eventually became incorporated into the expanding urban sprawl of Greater Manchester. Today it is a densely populated dormitory suburb of over 4,000 households, most of which are owned by their occupants. While not an affluent area, Timperley does not have deprivation issues and sits close to the national average according to education, health and wealth indicators.

Unfortunately for many residents, the Timperley Brook that drains part of the Mersey Basin runs through the town and has been identified by the Environment Agency of England and Wales as a 'Moderate' or 'Significant' flood threat, depending on topography, to the surrounding area. The Agency publishes online information for any householder to access in case they wish to check if their home is at risk from flooding. A 'significant risk' is one where a property-owner's chance of flooding each year is greater than 1.3 per cent (i.e. 1 in 75). There has been some investment in flood protection along the Brook, including a containment pond and an increase in the height of the banks, most recently in 2007. This was designed to reduce the chances of flooding in the event of excessive rain or rising river water. While there has not been severe flooding in the area for a generation, many older residents still remember the flood of 1981. Parts of the area often suffer minor or flash flooding when heavy rain overwhelms drainage systems, filling the cellars of some houses.

While the civil flood protection works may reduce the risk of damage to life and property, the threat remains. Unfortunately the Agency has not been successful in influencing residents, particularly owner-occupiers, to take action to protect their homes. They can do this by purchasing temporary barriers for the doors, fitting one-way valves to appliances that link to drains and other measures. But residents are not taking this advice. In fact, less than half (in concert with the rest of the country) have even agreed to sign up for the free flood warning service that the Agency offers to all households in flood-threatened areas (Bichard and Thurairajah, 2011). When the Agency approached me and my team at Salford University, it had been trying for some time to find a way to overcome this inertia. My work up to that time had focused on motivating and influencing for sustainable change, but I had been concentrating on trying to use behaviour change techniques to increase the uptake of energy-efficiency measures (insulation, heating units, efficient appliances, etc.) in domestic properties. However, there were strong parallels in applying these energy-related ideas to flood protection as they both required a type of transactional (one-off) behaviour change.

It was agreed that a series of studies, sponsored by the Agency in association with the local authorities of Salford and later Trafford, would be designed to discover if there was a combination of influencing measures or strategies that could solve the Agency's problem. In 2009, the research team conducted an attitudinal survey to see if the owner-occupiers of England and Wales connected climate change and risk to their home, and asked who they thought was responsible for protecting them against the damage that could be caused by global warming. The questions also probed the amount people knew about energy and flood protection measures, and asked if they would be tempted to invest, or invest more if they were offered an incentive. The incentives that were suggested were unusual ones. No cash reward was offered. Instead, an interest in non-cash rewards, including free fruit and vegetables, travel on public transport, access to further education, and free garden and landscape work, was tested out on the survey sample.

The inspiration for these non-cash incentives came from an initiative carried out some years earlier in a city in Brazil. The Green Trade Program was established in 1991 in Curitiba. The city was having difficulty collecting refuse from the unplanned outlying *favelas* or shanty towns, which housed the poorest people. To incentivise the population in these areas, the city bought surplus fruit and vegetables from farmers in the region and offered to give out the produce in exchange for an equal weight of recyclable waste. At its height the scheme was running food distribution/waste collection points in more than 75 locations across the city. The 7,000 people who participated benefited from approximately 44 tonnes of food every month. The city authorities say that not only did the waste problem improve but the poor benefited from a healthier diet and the farmers sold more of their crop (www.cbd.int/authorities/casestudy/curitiba.shtml).

The original survey in England and Wales, and later the local one in Timperley, found that the most popular non-cash rewards for investing in flood protection or energy saving were vouchers for fruit and vegetables (51.7 per cent of positive answers), followed by free meals at restaurants (44.2 per cent), tickets for entertainment (33 per cent) and vouchers for leisure and health centres (27 per cent). The least popular reward was free bus travel although the high proportion of over-60s who already have access to these services in England could explain this. Around a quarter of the people who answered the survey said they would not be persuaded to accept any value of rewards. But over 50 per cent said that they would accept rewards as long as they were worth at least as much as the amount they paid for the measures. A little less than half said they would participate in a reward scheme, should it be offered in their area.

The results from this work gave the Agency confidence that the idea could work in the field and the Salford team was asked to run a limited trial to test the proposition. Timperley was chosen as the trial site and the academic team looked for precedents on which to model the experiment. They were attracted to the work of the psychologist Paul C. Stern who had conducted studies over a 30-year period into sustainable decision-making (Stern, 2009). Stern saw that many of the contributory factors that influence decisions to adopt sustainable goods and services were counter-intuitive. He observed, for example, that non-financial factors are as important as financial ones. He also thought that if savings were used as an argument to induce behaviour change, it was important to know that consumers rarely treat actions that lead to efficiency as an investment.

Some of Stern's conclusions were more in line with common sense, although strategists often find them inconvenient. One example of this is that people economise on cognitive effort as well as money (i.e. they don't like to think hard for very long). Another is that inertia is a barrier to change (habits, risk aversion, etc.). Stern also endorsed the tactic of providing valid information from credible sources at the point that decisions are made. He recommended that strategists should keep the offer simple and provide quality assurance. The presence of the university logo on all material passed to the residents helped to reinforce the last point during the Timperley trial.

The trial design attempted to incorporate many of these principles, while maintaining a close association with the attitudes tested in the earlier parts of the study. This was achieved in a number of ways. The trial was based on a simple proposition offering rewards in return for adopting a few easy-to-understand energy and flood protection measures. The use of a green community group to communicate and facilitate the project helped to promote the understanding that this was a community project (as opposed to something the authorities or an energy company was imposing). The group made sure that residents knew they were representing the university, thus maintaining the all-important 'credible source' that Stern said was important. Interestingly, post-completion interviews still found that a proportion of residents said they were suspicious that the trial was just a cover for predatory power companies. In the previous decade high-pressure door-to-door selling campaigns had plagued many neighbourhoods as competing corporations tried to get householders to switch providers on their doorstep. Even though the community group agents made it clear that the trial had nothing to doing with this, the previous experience was strong enough for some householders not to take the risk of being taken in by untrustworthy sources.

The trial was designed in three parts. First, residents were visited by a green community group acting on behalf of the researchers who tested householders' attitudes toward climate change, attribution of responsibility and interest in investing in property-level measures in return for some non-cash rewards. Residents who expressed interest in the reward scheme were given a free combined flood and energy survey of their home. The residents were then invited to purchase some or all of the recommended measures in return for the rewards.

Each reward had an intrinsic sustainable value and was often linked to a social policy. For example, the landscaping reward was linked to a social enterprise that was running an offender rehabilitation scheme. The fruit and vegetable reward was justified as a way of improving the government's healthy eating targets. The public transport and adult learning rewards also fit with government objectives.

The trial involved a small sample of 50 homes to prove the concept was viable and so was never expected to produce large numbers of converts. About 20 per cent of those householders who accepted the home surveys went on to make a purchase and hence were eligible for the rewards. The five households that accepted the rewards chose fruit and vegetables, a season ticket for the tram (the light rail system for Manchester), a garden makeover and a beauty session at the local college in return for buying items including a new boiler, space heaters and insulation. The average spend by the residents was just over £1,000 while the cash value of the rewards was £840, showing that it is possible to motivate reluctant householders, promote social value initiatives, lower carbon emissions and provide measures at less than market prices.

Apart from showing that some people could be influenced by these unconventional methods, the study produced some other interesting and unexpected results. Half of the householders agreed to a full energy and flood audit. One energy company that spoke to the researchers was impressed with the ability of the team to get householders to open their doors to the auditors. Its representatives said that they achieved a response rate of less than 20 per cent for the same (energy) offer from their own customer base. There was also a recognition that engaging green community influencers was important as it gave confidence to those who participated in the later stages of the scheme that supportive assistance was always at hand. This reinforces the work of many others who have come to the same conclusion (Agyeman and Angus, 2003; Hoppner and Whitmarsh, 2011; John *et al.*, 2009).

At the end of the trial, the Salford team concluded that in order to convince doubtful home-owners that they needed to invest in occasional purchases that protected their property against climate change, three things needed to be in place: (1) an attractive incentive scheme; (2) information and support at the point when decisions are made; and (3) finally, a sense that people around them are at least as interested as they are in the proposition.

On completion of the study, the researchers and Action for Sustainable Living (AfSL), which was the green community group that helped deliver the trial for the university, reviewed the study. One conclusion was that while residents had commented on the value of having AfSL workers to help them, the group could have been even more effective. AfSL was happy to follow the researchers' instructions, but the way they interacted with the residents was not their normal mode of operation. If the group had approached the community on its own terms, it would not have offered residents a menu of fixed options to alter their houses, which was required by the design of the trial. Instead they would have had more open conversations, asking residents which particular issues concerned them about their environment. Once consensus is reached, they develop a programme to help the community to realise their own route to agency. Accepting this, for their part, the researchers were curious to see if the work they had started in the Timperley area would translate into more permanent (habitual) behaviour and the formation of an independent green community group.

As a result of this discussion, it was agreed that the university, in conjunction with Trafford Borough Council and other funders, would extend the presence of AfSL in the area to see if they could facilitate the new group. The first thing that AfSL did was to widen the catchment area as it considered that the original boundary, based on the Environment Agency's assessment of flood threat, did not include a viable number of households for their purpose. The group then started leafleting residents and invited them to express an interest in attending a meeting to discuss issues regarding the environment and their neighbourhood. But instead of directly mailing or handing out leaflets to adults, they enlisted the help of the local primary school and the invitations went home in the children's schoolbags.

The first meeting attracted about a dozen people, many more than the meetings called during the time the researchers were active in the area. They set up a Twitter account and an email list and interest started to spread throughout the rest of the community. Left to their own devices, the community did not elect to concentrate on energy or flooding, but chose food growing and tree-planting as their first projects. They focused on an old archaeological site that had fallen into disrepair, attracting anti-social behaviour. In a direct parallel to the Blacon Station project, the volunteers sought to rehabilitate the area and restore it to its former condition when it had been a popular open space. They began by fixing fences and planned out a new garden area. The new planting initially attracted local people who used to visit the area before it fell into decline. Word went around the neighbourhood and soon the area was being visited regularly by younger people and mothers with small children.

This project was followed by a series of composting workshops organised by a resident who had volunteered to be the community waste ambassador, and a scheme that promoted recycling and reuse. The community lobbied the council to provide new land to build allotments for all those people who said they were interested in growing their own fruit and vegetables. During the six-month initiative a dedicated AfSL community worker spent 15 hours a week with volunteers and more money was found for the school to engage children in other environment-focused exercises and projects.

The AfSL formula relies on self-suggested ideas which bring community members together in the belief that the more people talk to each other about their concerns, the more confident they become in collectively overcoming environmental problems. By the time the funding for the extension initiative in Timperley ran out, there were three constant members of the 'Sustainable Timperley' group and 12 more who said they would always respond to requests for help on particular projects when needed.

Occasionally AfSL find that an outstanding community leader emerges from their initial invitations. These individuals have the confidence and ability to come forward and galvanise their neighbours. But they also understand this type of person does not commonly present themselves and mostly they find that people need support, training and the confidence to go out and persuade their neighbours to join with them to promote their local environment. This takes courage and there is a need to overcome the fundamental problem that many people have which is a worry about how they will be regarded if they act outside the usual behaviour patterns of their community.

AfSL run a volunteer support scheme for all of their projects in a manner similar to those supporting social workers or bereavement councillors. The scheme ensures that those volunteering to organise their communities do not suffer from the constant strain of trying to influence others who, for a wide range of reasons, resist their invitations to act in an environmentally supportive manner. Not only does this work bolster confidence and understanding within their volunteer network, but it also means that they can tap the experiences of many different communities. AfSL has now run over 100 community projects, but they always ensure that all of their volunteers are in constant touch with each other.

AfSL has focused on the belief that any problem can be overcome when a minority turns to a majority, regardless of institutional or political intransigence. This certainly fits with what social psychologists suggest is part of a combined strategy to influence sustainable change. Nevertheless it is an extraordinary belief, and one which deserves further investigation to understand the motivation that drives this group. In 2001, Chris Wright ran a workshop called 'What Can I Do?' He had been thinking for some time about the implications of climate change and resource depletion with increasing irritation as he observed that those around him did not share his concerns. His vision was to bring people together at about a dozen at a time so that they could share their impressions of how the environment was being affected by modern society. The workshops were designed to help people put together individual action plans to improve their own lives and the lives of those around them. He systematically led the group through a definition and understanding of the existing local and global problems, the value changes required to improve the situation and the things that would need to happen to underpin significant change. Chris drew on his training in consensus building to do this and met with modest success in attracting a small number of people to share his sense of urgency.

However, Chris's satisfaction with this small project was short-lived. One of the people he had invited to join in the workshops questioned the impact he was having on both local and global change. The man pointed out that even if he ran a workshop every week, he would only be reaching a handful of people in the Greater Manchester area where he was based, never mind the rest of the country and beyond. Chris invited him to sit down with him to work out how more people could be reached. He then talked to some of his local government contacts and started canvassing opinions on how to roll out his idea. He started at his local food co-operative where he quizzed customers about their interest in participating in a wider community group.

He also sought and was successful in attracting modest amounts of money for his first community project which was a green community group in the primarily middle-class progressive neighbourhood of Chorlton. His ideas began to attract attention and projects in more challenging communities followed. A central government grant from the Department of the Environment (DEFRA) allowed him to expand into the communities of Hulme and Old Trafford (in the shadow of the Manchester United football stadium). As a result, he found that he could start to employ more people, including some badly needed project co-ordinators which he allocated on a ward-by-ward basis.

Another moment of reflection made him realise that although he was being successful on a wider scale, his efforts were very resource-intensive, requiring face-to-face and door-to-door interaction. He started wondering again about the scalability of his new model. He needed to spend less while engaging more people to make the grant money he received work more effectively. Talking to his community workers and volunteers, Chris then hit upon a new way of organising his programme by shifting to a community co-ordinator system. Volunteers were asked to commit to working eight hours a week for six months as Local Project Managers. They were recruited, trained and supported to do the ward-by-ward and face-to-face work. This freed up the more experienced (and paid) community co-ordinators to cover up to 12 different projects at the same time. Local Project Managers are now trained and supported to initiate their own projects. In addition, they are encouraged to attend local planning and event meetings, give talks, recruit other volunteers and write articles for local media. The community co-ordinators are always on hand to support and advise members of their community. This was a form of organisation that could respond well to Paul Stern's advice to offer information at the point of decision-making.

Action for Sustainable Living later went beyond communities and into schools, adopting a 'whole school' approach where the children and the building and the teachers were simultaneously the focus of sustainable change. This further morphing of the formula is now spreading to social housing tenants with a new initiative; the 'Energy Academy' which has been set up to help tenants to assist other tenants to both reduce energy and consume fewer resources in the home.

It's an impressive record and AfSL holds a justly won reputation in the Manchester area for grassroots organisation and significant sustainable gain at community level. You might expect the instigator of such an organisation to exhibit the qualities that he himself suggested were present in the very few dynamic sustainable champions. But Chris does not really fit this description. He is a soft-spoken reflective man, modestly though assertively explaining the achievements of his organisation.

Chris started as a social worker and then graduated into local government social services management. This put him, at the time, in the midst of a major social policy shift in the UK known as 'care in the community'. The government had decided that people with mental health and learning disabilities who had been traditionally segregated and cared for in large institutions,should be integrated back into the community. While this policy was applauded in principle, many social commentators thought that it could have a detrimental effect unless it was properly resourced and carefully implemented. The fear was that local authorities and neighbourhood doctors who would have to accommodate and care for patients would not have the resources to do this, resulting in a heightened risk to the rest of the community.

Chris saw that the public sector was ill-suited to do this job and left his post to set up a company that offered the range of support that was needed to ensure the patients received the care they needed in their new situation. At its inception, with just a single partner, Chris built up the business and by the time he left it employed over 500 members of staff. The experience taught Chris a number of lessons. The first was that institutions do not work very well as instant motivators of people. You cannot just pin up a poster or give a rousing speech and expect to see an immediate change in employee attitudes. He realised that people who come to work need to be given time and space to take up new ideas or be inspired by a new mission. He understood that if an organisation wanted to effect change, then it was necessary for it to be value-driven and that the precursor to the adoption of collective values was training. Finally, he came to realise that while it is always hard at the start of a change programme to move large numbers of people quickly to alter the way they live and think, it is possible to move a minority to lead the way and recruit the rest along the way. He saw that the identification and cultivation of these early movers were the key to wider success.

Chris linked this broader understanding of societal change to something that had been in the back of his mind for a long time. He remembered reading an article in *The Ecologist* magazine that had made him realise that the way richer societies live could not be sustained in the future. The article was entitled 'A Blueprint for Survival' (Goldsmith *et al.*, 1972). Written by the magazine's proprietor, Edward Goldsmith and others, the work was born out of the growing environmental movement catalysed by the first Earth Day in 1970. Goldsmith's article, published in a special issue of *The Ecologist* in 1972, went on to sell a total of 750,000 copies when later re-printed in book format. Goldsmith himself was a contentious figure on other subjects, but was nonetheless highly influential in galvanising a new generation of environmental campaigners in the UK. Many attribute the founding of the modern British Ecology (now known as the Green) Party to the views expressed in 'A Blueprint for Survival'.

The essay explained in graphic detail the way industrialisation and agricultural practices were disrupting ecosystems, contributing to the failure of food supplies, exhausting resources and ultimately leading to the collapse of society. The work contains some unequivocal yet timeless statements such as: 'our task is to create a society which is sustainable and which will give the fullest possible satisfaction to its members. Such a society by definition would depend not on expansion but on stability.' That view was re-stated much more recently by Tim Jackson in his influential publication *Prosperity Without Growth?* (Jackson, 2009). The combination of the factual and the romantic is encapsulated in another statement in 'A Blueprint for Survival' when it recommends that humanity should seek a stable society which 'as well as removing the sword of Damocles which hangs over the heads of future generations, is much more likely than the present one to bring the peace and fulfilment which hitherto have been regarded, sadly, as utopian' (Goldsmith *et al.*, 1972: 160).

Chris was not alone in being profoundly affected by 'A Blueprint for Survival'. Jonathon Porritt, a former leader of the Ecology/Green Party, writing on his blog on the occasion of Goldsmith's death in 2009, said he was heavily influenced by Goldsmith's work. Porritt went on to head Friends of the Earth and later became Chair of the UK government's Sustainable Development Commission. He described 'A Blueprint for Survival' as a 'get real summons like no other' (Porritt, 2009). Haq and Paul (2012) consider, like many others, that the article thrust ecology to the forefront of global consciousness. They state that after 'A Blueprint for Survival' was published, 'ecology was not solely a field of science, it was a philosophy to live by, one that challenged the assumptions and practices of modern society'.

With this world-view simmering in his consciousness and his experiences in organising within the realm of community health, all that Chris needed now was a few dry runs before he was ready to step out and start his new sustainable community leadership role. He became involved in an early version of an alternative energy community group called Energy 21 and then participated in one of the early local exchange trading schemes (LETS) in Manchester. Originating in Canada, LETS allow the exchange of goods and services within a community without the need for money. Successful alternative money projects generally operate in a wide pool of diverse skills and ultimately the Manchester group was too small to sustain a viable economic unit. But the experience helped Chris to understand how people can co-operate outside the   status quo. Above all, he understood that change rarely comes from sitting around talking about a problem, it can only come from people doing things.

Inner-city America: environmental redemption in Larimer, Pittsburgh

Larimer is a neighbourhood in the US city of Pittsburgh. For decades, the area has been the epitome of post-industrial American inner-urban decay. However, while some areas across the USA are still struggling to find their way out of the mire, neighbourhoods like Larimer have been experiencing some success through a combination of internal resilience and some inspired partnerships. Many of their recent initiatives have resulted in pro-environment projects which seem at first glance to be out of place in a community where the alleviation of poverty is often the dominant driving force. However, on closer inspection, Larimer's green edifice has indeed been built on social justice foundations.

Environmental issues connected with social justice have some powerful precedents in the USA. Cesar Chavez's battle in California with the Delano grape growers is an early dispute that came to national prominence and led to boycotts outside supermarkets. The original complaint was that the company was spraying crops with pesticides while the migrant workers were still working in the fields. This was in 1965. Another was the 1978 campaign by the Love Canal residents in Niagara Falls, New York, who focused the public eye on the the folly of building housing on a toxic waste dump. A more cohesive and organised environmental justice movement took shape soon after this in the USA. It emerged from 'the growing recognition that people of color and people with low incomes, more often than other segments of the population, live and work in areas where environmental risks are high' (Ferris, 2002).

Single-issue campaigns like Delano and Love Canal were impressive and effective as they linked negligent companies to environment impacts and human rights and well-being. But they were a reaction to acute and often criminal acts. Neighbourhoods like Larimer are now reacting to chronic environmental influences that have built up over generations. Together with poverty and poor historic economic and planning decisions, the deteriorating health of underprivileged neighbourhoods often eats away at its capacity to regenerate.

Like many Pittsburgh neighbourhoods at the end of the nineteenth century, Larimer was a wealthy area with some impressive stone-built mansions. The next half-century saw an influx of predominantly Italian immigrants. At one time the tiny neighbourhood packed over 13,000 residents into one square kilometre of land. Until the 1960s, Larimer was known as Little Italy and boasted some of the best restaurants in town. But the area's fortunes were harmed first by the downturn in the city's fortunes and later by a misguided attempt to improve the East End.

Between 1970 and 1990, Pittsburgh lost 158,000 jobs and 289,000 residents (almost 50 per cent of the current population). Manufacturing jobs (including steel production) were particularly hard hit, collapsing from employing 28 per cent to just 12 per cent in less than a generation. Larimer's Italian-American population left en masse to be replaced by a smaller number of African-American occupants who struggled to find jobs in the flagging economy. Today just 1,700 residents are left, but their impact on the city is significant as collectively they have a poverty rate that is double the county average. Almost half the residents of the community are living at or below the poverty line and about the same number do not complete a high school education (ending at age 18).

The fall-out from this economic disaster is not hard to see when you walk around the neighbourhood. There are over 700 vacant lots in Larimer amounting to almost 40 per cent of the total land area, over half of which is owned by public bodies. The usual attendant drug culture and gang conflicts did not improve the attractiveness of the area which had become blighted by the 1980s. The deterioration in both the housing stock (with many vacant or condemned premises) and public spaces completed the miserable contextual picture of a failing community.

In recent years Larimer has benefited from help offered by a number of individuals and agencies who have taken an interest in its revival. However, the constant in the area is the Kingsley Association (www.kingsleyassociation.org). The organisation was first named Kingsley House after the Christian Socialist and Oxford University student Charles Kingsley, who is credited, along with Frederick Dennison Maurice, with founding the settlement house movement in the East End of London. It was opened on Christmas Day 1893 and aimed to help labourers working in Pittsburgh's Strip District, which was home to many of the city's steel and metal-working factories as well as the rail yards. As a result of the Industrial Revolution, some of the immigrant workers drawn to the mills and factories found themselves living in poverty and in need of assistance. The settlement houses that were set up in many cities by philanthropists and religious organisations who were inspired by the work of Kingsley and Maurice met these needs before the modern welfare state developed later in the twentieth century.

Kingsley House was not just a place of refuge and support. It pursued a wide programme of cultural, educational and social activities including boys and girls clubs, literary societies, lectures, concerts, a kindergarten, and science and reading classes. By 1900, it had outgrown its original location in the Strip and moved first to the Hill District, and then in 1923, after changing its name to the Kingsley Association, it settled in its present location in Larimer Avenue, East Liberty.

Fred Brown is in charge of Program Development at the Kingsley. Fred explains his duties to visitors with an enthusiasm that does not show a hint of fatigue even though he has explained this to a long line of fascinated visitors who regularly book in to hear him speak. He directs a range of community-led environmental projects that both enhance the capacity of residents and improve the fabric of the neighbourhood. A good example is a web-based program that focuses on educating individuals and communities about sustainability. He is rightly proud of this idea which forms part of the Imagine Larimer initiative. It combines tailor-written software with off-the-shelf SMART Board technology to help residents understand measures that will make their lives more sustainable and save them money. It is designed to teach the trade-offs (both in terms of cost and impact) of the different choices available to householders such as insulation, heating appliances, water-saving measures, monitors, etc. He is also leading an initiative called the Urban Leadership Institute, a community sustainability program focusing on preparing participants for careers in green technology. But Fred is particularly interested in making the buildings and green spaces of Larimer work in ways that improve both well-being and economic prosperity.

Fred's résumé is impressive. He has experience as a trainer, an environmental justice leader and a policy analyst, and has spent time as a visiting lecturer at local universities. He also trained judges who work in the juvenile courts and is qualified in conflict mediation and resolution. On top of that, he has served as director and executive director of non-profit-making organisations since 1987. He started his working career as a schoolteacher in the East End. He graduated to being a youth worker and gained a Master's degree in social work. When he trained in conflict resolution, he was hoping to become effective in bringing neighbourhoods closer together.

But as time went on, he became more and more disillusioned with the gang culture and violence he saw all around him. One night he was called to yet another fight and discovered a young man who had been badly injured. The youth had been shot for a second time in a six-month period. Fred visited the youth in hospital, and while he was there, he received a call on his cell phone warning him that the attackers were on their way back to finish the job. Fred had already held one young man in his arms and watched him die. It made him feel determined to arrest the cycle of violence. But after attempting to redirect the wounded youth to adjust his compass in life, he chose to ignore Fred's advice and continued along his existing trajectory. He was murdered within days of being released from the hospital. Soon after he heard this news, Fred resigned.

While he was considering his future, a friend asked him to get involved in a transport and equity project. Fred said he knew virtually nothing about transport, but he was assured that his advice would be valuable because he was well connected with the African-American communities that were the focus of the work. Despite his misgivings, Fred became interested in the project and learned how being located near to major roads could contribute to a lack of education attainment and ill health as a result of poor air quality. His commitment to social justice became re-energised when he made the link between environmental harm and its inequitable influence on the poor.

This led to a new assignment in Washington, DC, with the non-profit-making Transport Equity Network where he helped to influence public policy on routing and proximity to vulnerable areas. Eventually this work helped to revise the federal guidelines on public participation and transportation equity. His next move was to take up a Ford Foundation grant to attend an environmental justice programme which gave him valuable environmental leadership skills and introduced him to a number of other environment-related issues.

Fred has since become interested in the Transition Town (TT) movement. He likes the way it cuts through the sometimes tedious lead-up and red tape of other community engagement programmes and gets right down to interactions with members of the community. TT came from an idea by Rob Hopkins, a permaculture specialist with an interest in ecological design. While teaching in the small coastal town of Kinsale in the Irish Republic, Rob set his students the task of tracking down a sustainable living model or strategy that had been adopted by another town or city. When they came back empty-handed, he decided to work with them to design one from first principles for Kinsale.

When he moved to the town of Totnes in Devon, England, he developed this strategy further and created a model that any group could easily follow. The Transition Network website explains that, 'whether we like it or not, over the next decade or two, we'll be transitioning to a lower carbon future – essential because of climate change and because of diminishing supplies of fossil fuels (particularly oil)' (Transition Network, 2012). After setting out the consequences of remaining wedded to fossil fuels, the commentary on the site advises that 'the best place to start transitioning away from this unviable way of living is right within our own communities, and the best time is right now'.

There are now over 1,000 communities in over a dozen countries that are either officially registered or 'mulling' over the prospect of joining the network. There are many others that are unofficially following Hopkins' formula for sustainable living. In the UK, the most high-profile Transition Towns are associated, although not exclusively, with smaller towns like Totnes and Lewes in Sussex. Both have adopted their own local currency to help keep wealth from flowing out of the local economy. Totnes has been in the news for successfully trying to keep local small businesses going by resisting the establishment of chain store branches in the town. Costa Coffee was an example of a large business that accepted the town's wishes and withdrew a planning application to locate in the town.

It is true that in England many of the successful TT groups are located in the more affluent southern parts of the country. Not all attempts to start a TT group are successful and some fail to gather enough people or initiatives to be viable. There are those who say that the language of the permaculture ethos, with its references to peak oil and resource production and consumption, appeals more to better-educated communities. Those working in deprived areas can sometimes be dismissive of the TT way because they find it hard to convey the economic arguments and graphic depiction of impending difficulties to their audiences. However, the focus on future resource collapse and the present efforts to build local networks and self-sufficiency is something that all communities can understand.

Fred does not think that the language is a problem because he changes it to suit his audience. He says you can translate anything into the way your own community speaks. He could see that that while some of the TT rhetoric might not go down very well in Larimer, the basic ideas behind it were still sound. In his view, in a world where resources become scarce, poor people will always suffer in disproportionate numbers unless they can be empowered to higher levels of self-sufficiency. To this end, he became a Transition Town trainer and regularly holds workshops in Larimer and other communities using materials and ideas generated by the approach.

By the time he came back home to Pittsburgh and joined the Kingsley, Fred was ready to put his new understanding of the world into action. He started fairly modestly with a weatherisation (energy-saving retrofit) project for 20 people. This led to the Imagine Larimer project. He took inspiration from a strategy his Executive Director observed in Greensburg, Kansas, that was designed to help rebuild tornado-hit communities. His team combined geographic information system technology that embeds data into digital maps with a simple interactive whiteboard to help people to understand how introducing energy conservation and other sustainable innovation into their homes would not only improve their lifestyles but would also reduce their living costs. He recruited people to use the system through a group called the Urban Green Growth Collective. The Collective was set up to ensure that people from minority populations had the opportunity to shape the emerging urban (re)development projects that were starting to take shape in the area.

The Collective meets on a monthly basis and is attended by other local non-profits and residents organised into a range of sustainability issues from health to social ventures, women in the green economy and (due to Fred's influence) environmental justice.

The Transition Town talks are delivered both as part of the Collective's programme and elsewhere. People who were already destabilised by the downturn in the economy after 2008 wanted some indication that their area was not going to deteriorate further. They were often too poor or unwilling to move from their homes which meant that retrofitting (re-fitting existing buildings) was the only viable option to improve both living costs and environmental impact. Raising awareness through the Collective allowed Fred to encourage residents to use the system that was already set up in the Kingsley headquarters where the meetings took place.

Another line of programme activity within Fred's and the community's overall plan was to improve the open spaces. A new master plan was proposing to eventually demolish the sparsely populated buildings on the edge of the neighbourhood, allowing better-quality green space and playing fields to be established. Fred reasoned that it was better to have more sustainable housing concentrated in one place than try to treat badly constructed and maintained buildings across a wider area. The strategy has been to attract anybody displaced by the demolition programme into the central core of the community. Meanwhile, better parks and community gardens can be established where residents can take more pride in their neighbourhood and learn how to grow their own food.

An enthusiastic non-profit, GTECH has been working with Fred, the Kingsley and other Larimer supporters to establish temporary planting on the long-vacant derelict land. One plot attracted interest from a developer after years of being ignored simply because it sprouted a dense crop of sunflowers as a result of efforts by GTECH and 60 residents. The theory is that gardening not only increases cohesion and overcomes food deserts, but adds a buzz to the area and produces good photogenic stories for both the media and potential funders. GTECH has been skilled in attracting grants and awards for a string of other projects in the East End. This includes the 'Larimer Green Team', that helps maintain newly tended sites while learning about the new green economy.

By this time Fred was starting to forge links with Pittsburgh's large higher education sector. In 2011, Fred worked with students at the University of Pittsburgh's Mascaro Centre and persuaded the Pittsburgh chapter of Engineers for a Sustainable World to come to Larimer to teach six classes on sustainability as part of the afterschool programme at Kingsley's Junior Urban Leadership Institute (JULI). The visiting lecturers covered a range of issues including energy, food, the design of sustainable buildings, water use and waste management. Each class lasted about two hours and focused on practical skills. A few of the ideas that emerged from these sessions included ways to light basketball courts sustainably and new schemes to set up solar hot water units from refrigerator coils and make mushroom caves out of shipping containers.

Another recent development in Larimer is the Environment and Energy Community Outreach Center or EECO Center. This project is an energy-efficiency education and resource centre built on the site of an old petrol station. The EECO Center's community partners are the Larimer Consensus Group and the Green Team. It will be managed by Pittsburgh Community Services Inc. The $650,000 it took to build the project came primarily from a range of public sector and charitable foundation sources typical of this part of western Pennsylvania. Apart from the benefits that the meeting space will offer to the community, the EECO Center will also be an exemplar for those looking for a resource to explain how to rehabilitate vacant or 'brownfield' urban sites. This is particularly pertinent in a post-industrial city that has an astounding 22,000 vacant lots dotting the landscape.

Fred now wants to step up the improvements to existing buildings in the neighbourhood. Building on the Imagine Larimer work, he has started a block-by-block competition to see if incentives will motivate more people to improve the energy efficiency of their homes. Ultimately he wants to see a complete retrofit programme that will not only reduce Larimer's carbon footprint, but also bring down the cost of occupation in still troubled economic times.

Leveraging the success of Imagine Larimer and the Urban Leadership Institute, both funded by the Heinz Endowments, Fred was able to create a workforce development programme that focused on 'Building Performance Institute' certified Energy Auditors. The Kingsley was the first organisation to graduate an African American, non-incumbent auditor in the whole of south-western Pennsylvania. He has also trained residents in industrial mechanics, started a landscape co-operative and created a Micro Business Institute in partnership with Pittsburgh Community Services Inc. The PCSI website explains that it is devoted to support programmes and activities 'designed to enable and empower low-income residents to make measurable progress on the continuum from impoverishment to self-sufficiency'. The new Institute will train residents to be successful entrepreneurs.

Fred has also partnered with Carnegie Mellon University's Urban Build Design Studio where he is working with college students and community residents to design NetZero houses intended to be used in the Larimer Vision Plan. He is staging this work at the Urban Leadership Institute which is training residents to become retrofit builders. Each phase of work is intended to create a concurrent training opportunity for community members while enhancing their understanding of the environment.

In an interview in the local magazine *Pittsburgh City Paper* in 2012, Fred explained to the journalist that one of the projects that had been occupying him recently was a proposal to build 37 new low-income houses on Larimer Avenue. The Larimer Consensus Group successfully persuaded the developer to re-orientate the buildings so that they were south-facing in order to take advantage of solar gain and reduce heating bills in the winter. It was a small intervention trying to solve a big problem, but the story is typical of Fred's dual motivations of building a just and environmental sustainable community in Larimer.

In their concluding remarks of their report, *The Climate Gap* (Morello-Frosch *et al.*, 2009), the authors say that there is not enough investment in low-income communities to help them prepare for the consequences of climate change, a problem they term the 'climate gap'. They quote the British Stern Report (Stern, 2006) that states: 'Low income and minority communities could be more seriously harmed by the economic shocks associated with climate change both in price increases for basic necessities (i.e. water, energy, and food) and by threats of job loss.' The authors conclude by saying that more discussions led by skilled researchers and community workers in these communities will be required. Morello-Frosch *et al.* (2009) prescribe that:

> One of the first steps to addressing the climate gap is to tackle the conversation gap. This can be achieved by working together across sectors and constituencies and ensuring that the effects of climate change and climate policy are not experienced in an inequitable manner between the white wealthy and low income communities of color.

They say that this is 'exactly the recipe we need to cool the planet and create economic opportunities and health benefits for everyone'. It seems that the work that Fred Brown and Chris Wright are doing may well be bridging the conversation gap and ultimately the climate gap beyond.

6   Food

The great sustainability translator

Community greens

In 2009, Michelle Obama, the First Lady and wife of the President of the United States, dug up a piece of the historic White House lawn and started to grow vegetables there. Her motivation was the deterioration of childhood health, and obesity in particular, caused by poor diets (Obama, 2012). For many, this was a revelation. Not the concern about obesity, but digging up the sacred White House lawn. Home and community grow–cook–eat schemes have blossomed all across America as a result

But the history of urban community gardens in the United States goes much further back than the First Lady's efforts and has usually been associated with times of hardship and food insecurity. Peter Ladner (2011) points out that the Mayor of Detroit encouraged citizens to tend local potato patches in the city during depressions as far back as 1893. This idea was copied across the nation with government assistance known as 'work relief gardens' during the Great Depression in the 1930s. During the two World Wars of the twentieth century, citizens were encouraged to create 'Victory Gardens' on any available patch of ground. However, Ladner reveals that it was not until 1978 that the American Community Garden Association (ACGA) was set up with members across the USA and Canada.

The 're-birth' of the grow-your-own tradition in the 1970s may have started for a variety of reasons. Laura Lawson in her book, *City Bountiful* (2005), speculated that there may have been 'a resistance to urban abandonment, as well as to provide resources to address inflation, express a new environmental ethic, and re-connect neighbours during a time of social unrest'. Lawson adds that there are other examples across the country where reformers, naturalists and educators got behind urban horticulture to create jobs and skills, educate children about food and its origins, bring the natural world into degraded urban streetscapes, introduce renewed confidence to failing neighbourhoods and provide a focal point for community cohesion. However, if the pattern of threat or hardship preceding the interest in grow-your-own is correct, then the 1973–4 OPEC oil embargo on the USA will have persuaded many to consider food self-sufficiency.

While this small revival in the 1970s kept the community garden movement alive, it could not really be considered in the same league as the mass participation pastime seen in European countries. Lawson points out that a survey in 1996 by the ACGA found that less than 6 per cent of community gardens in 38 cities were secured by permanent ownership agreements. It was still common then for public or private interests to claim the land back for development although she says this was often prompted by a fall-off in interest from those using the sites to grow crops. Writing before Michelle Obama's historic transformation of the White House lawn, Lawson suggests that with the 'multi-functionality' and patchwork justifications for community planting, the purpose of a community garden was not always clear. In recent times, the majority of North American society has been used to plentiful and relatively cheap food. The co-incidence of national leadership and yet another economic downturn in 2007–8 may have re-focused American minds to reinvent the motivation to become more in tune with food production and distribution by taking matters – literally – into their own hands.

However, while much of the new experience in America is about the rediscovery of growing your own produce, some communities are seeing the potential of food as a vehicle to teach aspects of self-sufficiency and regeneration. One strand of thinking relates to the spread of communal planting and harvesting as a mechanism for a wider conversation about how everyone can participate in keeping the community going. Some of these projects will be explored later in this chapter.

Another strand has been the establishment of wholesome, cheap food where previously there was none. These ideas centre on the ability of the community to come together and to lobby for, plan for and raise funding for better food retail opportunities, leading to the inevitable health, local economy and cohesion benefits. Many of the best examples of this are occurring in inner-city America as it is only in the past ten years that many city authorities have started to become effective at tacking decline in these areas. Some have focused on bringing the rural to the urban rather than relying on state benefits venturing outside their neighbourhood in search of higher-quality, cheaper food. This has led to a revival of the Farmers Market movement and some innovative food retail ideas.

Rural to the urban

There is nothing particularly novel in the efforts of the producers of goods to make the journey from point of production to the point of demand. Sanderson *et al.* (2005) collected a wide range of sources to describe the history and purpose of the farmers markets in North America. Market-day gatherings in towns were a European tradition that came over with successive waves of immigrants to North America. Research shows that the first documented farmers market in America dates from the seventeenth century. By the nineteenth and early twentieth century, markets selling farm products in centres of population were the most common way for urbanites to buy food. The economic viability of these markets should have been stable; except that the towns that collected stall rents from the retailers did not always reinvest the funds back into the infrastructure of the market places.

In many places, the buildings and lands used to house the markets were in a poor state of repair and the small profits made from the rents meant that public investment either in the fabric of the market or in its management (thereby allowing the businesses to be more successful) could not be justified to the taxpayer. There was undoubtedly both a social and an economic value in maintaining a common meeting place where people from different areas could congregate and make new deals that would create wealth and jobs in the future. However, this would have been an intangible benefit to those looking for more clear-cut evidence to justify public expenditure.

The need to maintain a common central meeting place like a market diminished by the middle of the twentieth century as urban living became more populous and more complex. The demand for more than one food retail site led to the development of local economic centres with their own supply chain arrangements. This increased the mobility of the population in search of food retail opportunity and made the modern supermarket inevitable. This in turn further undermined the demand for Farmers Market-types of shopping and with it the direct link between the shopper and the producer.

Modern food logistics chains stretch across the entire globe, taxing buyers to recognise the country of origin, let alone the region or the farm that grew or produced the item. In carbon emission terms, the distance food travels before it arrives at its final retail point is not as significant as the way the food was produced. Weber and Matthews (2008) showed that food miles were, on average, responsible for about 4 per cent of a shopper's carbon footprint while the nature of the food (and red meat in particular) had a much more significant impact. However, other factors, such as the potential interruptions of logistics chains because of fuel shortages or severe weather due to climate change, the retention of money in local economies and the role of food as a local and regional identifier, also justify the investment in locally produced food.

The modern Farmers Market revival in the USA coincided with the interest in community gardening in the 1970s. Today the United States Department of Agriculture (USDA) estimates that there are almost 8,000 farmers markets in US towns and cities. Sanderson *et al.* (2005) have considered the modern advantages of these markets to the potential regeneration of local economies and neighbourhoods. The access to fresh food, particularly for low-income inner-city residents, can be important, particularly where supermarket operators have pulled out of deprived areas.

The mixing effect that was so important for commerce centuries ago has now become significant again for different reasons. Cultural cohesion, elusive in some cities where mistrust and rivalry between communities sometimes boils over into unrest, is encouraged around the markets that sell a range of ethnic foods that attract multicultural shoppers. There is also the re-discovery of the consumer–producer bond because the seller is also the grower and can vouch for the provenance of the food and explain how to prepare and store it. Other advantages are food security, community identity and partnership opportunities between businesses.

Eating the way to better neighbourhoods

Communities have used food in different ways to help improve the economic fortunes of their area. High-quality, locally available food retail opportunities can be hard to find in deprived areas. Typically communities need to wait until a regeneration initiative improves the standard of housing, the public realm and increases the disposable income levels of the general population before retailers are prepared to invest in an area. But occasionally a community that is alive to the importance of food both for the health of its population and to improve inward investment comes up with a winning formula.

In 2000, the natural and organic food retailer Whole Foods Market (WFM) established a new store in the deprived Pittsburgh neighbourhood of East Liberty. At that time there was just one other grocery store (Giant Eagle) serving not just East Liberty, but the whole East End of Pittsburgh. As a result of this unlikely decision, the next ten years saw three more food retailers locating within a kilometre of the WFM store. The four retailers now generate well over $250 million in annual sales. But there are several other benefits that have come from the location of WFM. The neighbourhood now hosts a monthly farmers market, and the community has taken an interest in a number of new environmental and urban agriculture projects.

East Liberty boasted the third largest shopping district in all of Pennsylvania less than 50 years ago. In 1959, the area specialised as a garment district and hosted 575 businesses in the midst of a local population of almost 14,000. In the 1960s, city planners thought they could attract more people into the area by re-routing traffic around the business district. The idea was a disaster and had the opposite effect, effectively destroying the fabric of the community. The existing street grid was replaced by street-level car parks which stood unused and over the next 15 years the district lost over 300,000 square metres of commercial space. Blight spread into the neighbouring communities of Friendship, Bloomfield and Garfield, and crime rates rapidly increased. At its lowest point, local businesses were down to less than 100 units and the population dropped to below 6,000.

In 1979, the East Liberty Chamber of Commerce formed the non-profit community development organisation East Liberty Development, Inc. (ELDI) to facilitate redevelopment efforts in the neighbourhood and begin the process of reversing the effects of urban renewal. The organisation's first projects in the early and mid-1980s focused on improving the main shopping streets of the district. But by the end of the 1990s, although many projects had been completed, the underlying problems remained. Statistics from the 2000 Census showed that 14.4 per cent of the 4,121 homes in East Liberty were vacant and a large part of the population was transient with 81.5 per cent rented occupancy, compared to 48 per cent throughout the rest of Pittsburgh (ELDI, 2010). The economic indicators were no better with about 30 per cent of the population at or below the poverty line in 2000 and 2008. After 20 years of trying, ELDI was still having a hard time attracting investors because the neighbourhood was perceived as unsafe and the workforce degraded. In 2000, the unemployment rate was 11.1 per cent, twice the rate of the surrounding metropolitan area.

ELDI decided to review what was going wrong with their attempts to revive the area, and with the aid of advisors they noticed that while East Liberty showed continuing signs of decline during the 1990s, the three adjoining neighbourhoods were improving. Each had more than 100,000 people who were earning over $81,000 and over half of their population were educated to degree level. Intuitively ELDI had been trying to revive the area in the centre or commercial core of the district. But they came to realise that they should have been concentrating on the fringes close to the more affluent neighbourhoods. These people might have been worried about venturing into the heart of an unknown environment, but would be quite happy to cross a boundary street to visit an attractive store. When a Home Depot opened up in East Liberty in 2000, it attracted wealthier shoppers and this helped to calm nerves about whether this theory would turn out to be true.

The next piece in the puzzle was to find the right retailer, and at the time there was really one obvious contender. Whole Foods Market started with one small shop in Austin, Texas, in 1980. Currently it now has over 300 stores in the USA and the UK, employing over 60,000 people and amasses gross annual sales of more than $9 billion. The company grew largely through a continual process of mergers and acquisitions and maintains core values that include support for organic farmers, environmental protection and 'to be active participants in our local communities'. The company says it gives a minimum of 5 per cent of its profits every year to a wide variety of community and non-profit organisations (WFM, 2013). In 2010, it launched a programme called 'Health Starts Here'™ which includes classes, store tours and in-store centres focused on healthy eating choices and cooking ideas.

The WFM brand had, throughout the time it had been expanding in the 1990s been most at home in neighbourhoods with higher levels of disposable incomes. It would not have required a retail analyst to work out that East Liberty would not fit this mould. However, a local developer, the Mosites Company, recognised the opportunity and contacted ELDI to ask if it could help to attract Whole Foods Market to a site on the edge of the central retail district. At the time, the site contained only a few businesses including a car wash and a taxi cab company. The two parties drew up a development plan and the cost of the project ultimately totalled $7.6 million. The project would require a substantial amount of site preparation and infrastructure improvements and the all-important agreement from WFM to take a risk and open up in unfamiliar surroundings.

Yet, improbably, that is precisely what came to pass and when the Whole Foods Market store opened on 17 October 2002, it was an immediate success. Its opening day sales were among the highest ever reported for the Whole Foods chain. This would later be regularly exceeded as the reputation of the store gained fame in the following months. The business was so successful that by December 2003 there were 249 employees, 100 more than expected in the original business plan. A breakdown of employees showed that 56 per cent were from low-income communities, 63 per cent of the jobs paid more than the minimum wage and all jobs offered benefits and profit sharing, showing that the ELDI strategy to encourage good local jobs was working.

According to the branch manager, when WFM opened (and for five years afterwards), the branch had the highest rate of Access Card usage in their chain. Access Cards were formerly known as food stamps which are food credits for people below the poverty line and who are consequently receiving state benefits. The WFM deal was important for the regeneration of East Liberty because it established a quality food retailer in a deprived area, but it also gave confidence to the market to continue to invest after the initial breakthrough. As soon as the Whole Foods Market project was agreed, ELDI moved to acquire adjacent sites for future development. Over the next ten years, these new retail units have housed a spa, a premium wine and beer retailer, a large Trek bike store and a number of household-name chain stores. In addition, many new restaurants have been established in the streets adjacent to the retail sites across a range of affordability. There are now more jobs in East Liberty than people of working age, making East Liberty a net importer of labour. Commercial development has generated 849 new jobs in East Liberty since 1999, in addition to construction jobs created by new build projects.

Later, ELDI would come to understand that there were four factors that came together to contribute to the success of the project. These were:

1. a committed private developer willing to assemble a complicated development site and work with unusual sources of public and third-sector funding (the Mosites Company);
2. support from the public sector to provide the infrastructure platform for WFM to open (traffic access, lighting, etc.);
3. WFM recognising that while the store was located in a 'distressed neighbourhood', it adjoined more wealthy neighbourhoods which offered the potential to attract better shopper demographics into the area;
4. a compelling story about East Liberty, as told largely by local community groups, East Liberty Development, Inc. and the developer.

This last element was a key component in giving investors, and particularly the charitable donors and lenders, the confidence to back the project. Significant donations and loans came from a variety of organisations including the McCune, Hunt, Pittsburgh and Richard King Mellon Foundations and the Heinz Endowments.

The existence of ELDI created a focal point that allowed regeneration money from the city (via a vehicle called the East End Growth Fund, EEGF) to pump-prime a range of community initiatives that were collectively supported by the whole community. Other parts of the city were not so lucky and had fragmented representative groups who competed for the modest sums offered up by the administration. The Growth Fund helped East Liberty to establish its community plan, a participative visioning exercise, as early as 1999. The Fund was structured to make sure that ELDI owned property or the rights to buildings which allowed it to have a regular income long after the grants and loans had run their course. This return on their investment allowed the company to grow their capacity and invest in new ventures. This investment power also helped to leverage influence over developers to hire local people to staff the businesses that were being housed in the new commercial space.

The influence of the WFM deal has gone well beyond the classic boundaries of economic regeneration for the community. A few years after the store was established, WFM encouraged a farmers market to take place on a regular basis on a part of the store's car park. This is an independently organised market and is not part of the city-wide network. It also found the community receptive to its community garden initiative. In East Liberty, a member of staff from the store helped to manage the Enright Park Community Garden three blocks away. The gardeners benefited from assistance on planting, composting and growing techniques and this led to a partnership with the Kentucky Avenue elementary school. The pupils have also had lessons on growing and harvesting their own food which is then cooked and consumed as part of the 'Living Lunch' programme which is supported with donations from WFM.

How to make the desert bloom

Meanwhile, across town in another deprived area, the same problem was being tackled in another way. In the autumn of 2004, a Master's student from Pittsburgh's Carnegie Mellon University's Urban Design program sat in on a community meeting in the Hill District, north of the central core of the city. Residents were ruing the fact that there were no volume food retailers in the area and anything other than cheap white bread and fast food was hard to find or was too expensive to buy. In fact, the Hill District had not had a full-service grocery store in the area for nearly 30 years. One of the suggestions was that it might be possible to organise access to better food themselves by forming a food co-operative.

This gave the student an idea and soon colleagues from the Business School and public administration courses got involved. In 2005, they won the prestigious JP Morgan Chase Community Development Competition with a project entitled 'Center Food: Bringing a Non-Profit Food Store to Pittsburgh's Hill District Neighborhood'. As part of the award, a non-profit organisation called the Hill House was given $25,000 to expand on the students' ideas and develop a plan to attract a food retailer to the area. To date, the community has secured land and a trader that will lease a new building which will be owned by the community.

The funding was made possible through the innovative use of a Community Benefit Agreement and contributions from other parties. The plan is to build a shopping centre which will include a grocery store with a bakery and a delicatessen. The opening date is currently scheduled to be autumn 2013. The enabling mechanisms for the Hill District supermarket are important to understand in this story, but there are broader issues for all green community projects to learn. This is particularly true for communities that have ambitions to establish a large built environment project. Larger investment tends to be made as a result of personal drive, persistence and the right connections. But it can sometimes rely on the ability to access the right type of help at the right time.

In the 1840s, the Hill District was a wealthy neighbourhood overlooking the centre of the town of Pittsburgh. Just over 100 years later it had been occupied by successive immigrant groups culminating in a predominance of African Americans attracted from the southern US states with the promise of work in the thriving industries of the city. Hill District became known as a centre for jazz and many well-known artists including Charlie Mingus, Sarah Vaughn, Lena Horne, Oscar Peterson, Miles Davis, John Coltrane, Dizzy Gillespie, Cab Calloway and Duke Ellington entertained in venues in the area.

By the end of the Second World War over 90 per cent of the buildings were deemed to be sub-standard and in 1955 a federal slum clearance plan demolished large areas of the Lower Hill part of the district. The plan knocked down over 1,300 buildings and displaced more than 1,500 families (8,000 residents in total) and 400 businesses (Ferman, 1996). Much of this land was used to build a new civic arena which was completed in 1961. The intention was to move the central business district closer to the Hill for the benefit of the community. It did not work. Between 1950 and 2000, the Hill District lost 78 per cent of its population. Riots after the assassination of Martin Luther King in 1968 caused damage to many remaining buildings and further undermined the reputation of the area. The majority of present-day residents now live in public housing located north and south of the main commercial district. Approximately 20 per cent of the private housing units are vacant and the median income is less than $15,000.

During the 1960s residents began to fight back and challenge further plans to redevelop the area. In 1963, the Citizens Committee for Hill District Renewal, an umbrella group representing 40 organisations, was formed to oppose the 'top-down' planning process. Primarily the groups focused on proposals for another grand project (a new cultural centre) and offered a counter-proposal for new housing and the rehabilitation of much of the existing stock. The cultural centre was never built, but the residents did not get many of their own demands through either.

In the past 15 years there have been some signs of improvement in the Hill. The Urban Redevelopment Authority has spent $242 million to clear poor housing and replace this with both subsidised and market-rate dwellings, resulting in roughly 1900 new homes. However, the poverty levels and the loss of much of the area's economic infrastructure have continued to hinder regeneration efforts. Many businesses have found trading conditions very difficult and have closed, including all of the large food retailers. This led to what regeneration practitioners and health professionals call a food desert. The Department of Agriculture (USDA) favours the Healthy Food Financing Initiative (HFFI) definition of food deserts as a 'low-income urban area where at least one third or at least 500 people live more than a mile from a supermarket' (HFFI, 2010). HFFI say that around 23 million Americans live in areas which are only served by fast food restaurants and convenience stores that have limited healthy eating options.

As 60 per cent of the population in the Hill District do not own a car, reaching fresh healthy food can be difficult for many people. Most have to take a bus to travel to surrounding districts in order to buy fresh fruit and vegetables and other healthy foods. In 2000 (according to census data), there were 11,853 people in the five sections of the Hill District, showing that the area represents a willing market for retailers.

Unlike East Liberty, bodies that represent the interests of Hill District residents did not coalesce into a single lobbying force. Instead, and similar to many other areas, representation has divided along geographic, faith, political and ethnic lines. The Hill District Community Plan of 1996 listed the Hill Community Development Corporation, Hill Ministries, the House of the Crossroads, Hill District Federal Credit Union and the Hill House Association as well as a number of individual (independent) activists as contributing to the discussions about the future of the area (Stoker and Robert, 1996).

This changed in 2007 when the community began to organise. Two separate coalitions emerged from this. One Hill was formed by over 100 community organisations, including block clubs, faith groups, social services agencies and businesses. The other coalition was called the Hill District Consensus Group. This was comprised of residents and community organisations. This coalition had the financial support of Pittsburgh United, a group of church, union and community activists committed to securing economic justice for communities.

Redwood and Young-Laing (2012) explain that both groups were concentrated on plans to construct a new arena for Pittsburgh's professional ice hockey team, the Penguins. The site for this was adjacent to the old civic area that was responsible for devastating the district 40 years previously. Even though it was a long time ago, the community memory of this was still raw. In return for agreeing to stay in the city, the owners of the hockey club received $15 million of credit toward buying the land, the provision of a new arena and the rights to retain receipts for all the concerts, parking money and naming rights associated with arena. In return, the club has to pay the city $4.2 million a year.

During the negotiations between the city and the club, Hill District communities were considering how they could use a new legal instrument designed to ensure that communities gain some benefit from development that affects their area. A Community Benefits Agreement (CBA) is a private contract negotiated between a prospective developer and community representatives. Its development coincided with the move, from about the late 1990s, to regenerate inner-city areas commonly suffering from under-investment and attendant socio-economic problems such as high crime rates, low educational attainment and health disparities.

The CBA specifies the benefits that the developer will provide to the community in exchange for the community's support for its proposed development. The agreement usually contains a list of requirements often including a sum of money from a private developer that is seeking public funds. The driver for the agreement lies in the recognition that the developer must win the support of the local people before construction can commence. The public funding may be in the form of subsidies or relocation grants to attract the developer into an area, or it could be as result of the authority offering funding to augment or enhance the original proposal.

Because of the public financing element in the plans to develop the new arena, the community was able to make a case for a CBA. However, discussion about the breadth of the community coalition that would control the CBA led to a lack of consensus between the various groups and almost led to a failure to secure the agreement at all.

The terms of the Hill District CBA stated that the parties should provide funding to build a full-service food store with a pharmacy trading in a minimum of 25,000 square feet and that the asset (land and buildings) should be retained by the community.

Eventually, after a lot of wrangling, demonstrations and court challenges, the CBA was signed on 19 August 2008. In addition to the store, the agreement mandated the developer to hire local people for a variety of jobs. About 40 per cent of the 522 full- and part-time jobs created at the new arena and 73 per cent of the jobs at the Cambria Suites Pittsburgh hotel next door were subsequently given to people from the Hill District or people who attended local jobs centres that were created as part of the agreement.

The deal was worth $8.3 million to the community. To expedite the plans to build the new supermarket, the Urban Redevelopment Authority paid $1 million out of a capital fund which was then matched by the Penguins organisation. The Hill House Association was given the responsibility to implement the project and to use the $2 million of CBA money to leverage the remainder of the construction costs.

The Hill House has a long history in the district, stretching back over 100 years when two of its predecessor agencies (the Anna B. Heldman and the Soho Settlement Houses) helped European immigrants, and later Jewish settlers, to adapt to their new lives in Pittsburgh. These organisations played the same role as the Kingsley which was also located in the Hill District for a time. All these settlement houses acted as support networks in the absence of any organised state social security system. During the 1960s, when resident action in the Hill District was becoming stronger, a new social agency was formed out of the settlement house tradition to confront these problems. Known as the Hill House, the organisation joined the settlement houses with youth groups to offer lessons of leadership to young people.

Drawing from the roots and values of the settlement house concept, the Hill House Association was the first agency to combine health, welfare, recreation and community programs in the District. In 1970, the Hill House Housing Development Corporation (now the Hill House Economic Development Corporation) was formed and became one of the first agencies to tackle housing redevelopment on the Hill. Two years later the organisation completed a new headquarters on Centre Avenue and worked to bring other agency partners into the building, forging a collaborative spirit across the area. More recently, in 1997, Hill House began its first-ever capital campaign and raised $5 million to renovate its campus facilities. Today, the Association's website claims that the organisation serves over 70,000 people a year on matters including housing, skills and health (www.hillhouse.org/home.html).

While Hill House was used to receiving donations and grants for its social programmes, raising capital was more difficult. Built environment projects in the past had been almost exclusively focused on social housing provision, so when discussions started on solving the food desert problem, Hill House did not have much of a track record to call upon.

With the $2 million from the CBA, Hill House and its partners went about task of securing the remainder of the funds needed to build the supermarket. They were successful in attracting the McCune Foundation, the Heinz Endowments, the Richard King Mellon Foundation and the Pittsburgh Partnership for Neighborhood Development to provide the remainder of the funding. In February 2009, Hill House Development Corp. took possession of the land for the new store.

However, it took until July 2012 for the chain retailer Shop 'n Save to agree to trade out of the proposed new supermarket building. The original business plan forecast the employment of 100 people in a store that would support a bakery and a deli. The plan put the total cost of the project at $8.5 million. Shop 'n Save does not operate in the same market as Whole Foods Market. It is a franchise business that generally locates in lower-income neighbourhoods where budget retail strategies are successful. Nevertheless, Jeff Ross, the franchisee who agreed to trade out of the Hill District store, stated that he was prepared to operate the business at that site according to the wishes of the community. However, he said he could not do this without the $7.5 million in financial support from public and third-sector sources. The operator's stake was to be $1 million in start-up costs. He had previously operated similar food retail businesses over 35 years and had four other Shop 'n Save stores under his management at the time he agreed to take on the store in Pittsburgh.

However, four years after the initial CBA was announced, only the site-development work had been completed on the land at Centre Avenue and Heldman Street. The project had spent over $3 million, thus accounting for about 42 per cent of the original committed funds and the total cost of the project began to extend beyond the secured funding. The development is now predicted to cost a total of $9 million by the time it opens. The project's funders stopped spending until a new plan was put in place to complete the project and the exact amount of the funding shortfall was calculated. Hill House has accepted that project management issues had delayed the project, but that should not detract from the overall merit of the original idea. It was a project that was always worth fighting for.

In November 2012, the *Pittsburgh Business Times* reported that the first Vice Chair of the Hill House Board of Directors had confirmed that the funding gap for the project had been closed and that the development would act as an anchor for at least four other businesses in the complex (Coyne, 2012). The Association said it hoped that the store would be opening in the Spring or Summer of 2013, creating 100 jobs. At the same time the Mayor of Pittsburgh, Luke Ravenstahl, announced the re-development of the New Granada Theatre site further down Centre Avenue from the new Shop 'n Save. He said that the scheme will include a 51-unit residential and a retail complex. It appeared from the mayor's news that the same domino effect that helped East Liberty to revive was starting in the Hill District. More important, the Hill District's less wealthy citizens were finally going to get a place where they could buy some decent food.

The Boston Tree Party

Lisa Gross is the Chairman and Founder of the Boston Tree Party (http://www.bostontreeparty.org). She is an artist who works in the field of social practice/social sculpture. Her cross-disciplinary projects create opportunities for learning, connection and multi-sensory engagement. Reading this on the website makes Lisa's ideas sound intriguing and justifiably so. The Boston Tree Party is, on the face of it, an urban orchard scheme. But like Lisa's résumé, it works on many different levels. At first glance, Lisa's qualifications do not really match the profile of a grow–cook–eat activist and yet she is in the forefront of a rapidly growing movement to use food as force for community development. In less than two years (the initiative took off in the Spring of 2011), the 'Party' has now planted hundreds of apple trees and has signed up over 70 communities, or delegations as they are known, from all over the Greater Boston area. They include schools, universities, assisted living centres, community groups and businesses. Its goal is to produce 15,000 free heirloom apples a year by the fourth year of its existence.

She chose apples for a number of reasons. There is a connection between apples, health and well-being. There is also a connection with Boston. Apples were first planted in America at Beacon Hill by William Blackstone. The first American variety of apple, the Roxbury Russet, was also cultivated in the area. Indeed, students of Boston's green city credentials might assume that an urban orchard is something to be expected in a place that hosts one of the country's oldest community gardens. However, a tour and talk with people who are responsible for the Fenway Community Garden point out that for almost a century the tenants used their plot like the back garden they could not have because they were apartment dwellers. Even today there is a wide variety of hedges, shrubs, flowers and even water features found in the plots in the Garden, but very little fruit or vegetables.

This deeper understanding about the city's apparent disassociation with urban horticulture makes Lisa's idea sound risky. But when she launched her initiative in a gusty urban park, she told her audience an interesting fact about apple trees; apples (in common with many other fruit trees) cannot reproduce on their own – they need a different tree to pollinate the blossom in order for them to bear fruit. She goes on to say this is a trait shared in a different way with human beings; people must cross-pollinate ideas to be successful and this accentuates our interdependence. She tells the audience that we need to seek out and value diversity because 'that's how you get the sweetest and juiciest fruit' (Gross, 2011). A year on, in a recent film made by Jennifer Kelly, Lisa explains that the Party has three strands to its mission. It is, at the same time, a 'participatory public art project'; an 'urban agriculture project'; and a 'performative re-imagining of American political expression'. She says that 'delegates' ask permission to plant the fruit trees in a civic space while promoting the fruits of civic engagement (Kelly, 2012).

There are many potential outcomes of this unusual act. The trees can help to control urban flooding. They offer safe food as air pollution is absorbed into the tree but not the fruit. They provide a sense of place for both the planters and those who come to see them as a local landmark. They have an aesthetic quality but also are practical providers of shade. They represent a small fight back against the food desert and are a focus for discussions in deprived areas about regeneration ideas. They represent a badge of membership to encourage other delegates to visit each other and share stories. Lisa would also add that the idea represents an intersection between social art (celebrating the structure and symbolism of the trees) and the encouragement of social entrepreneurial activity where people organise together for a successful project.

The proposition and offer behind the Boston Tree Party is simple. Each delegation receives a Tree Party Kit with everything they need to plant and grow two apple trees. The Party then provides support and workshops to delegates, staffed by gardening education organisations and in-house pomologists. The care and maintenance need to be low cost and tailored to allow each group to create its own project, according to its needs and interests. Many groups find a spare patch of lawn outside a school or church, but some are more imaginative. The East Boston Neighborhood Health Center near

Logan Airport created their community garden on an abandoned car park, breaking through the asphalt in order to find the soil underneath.

The Party is also proud of a delegation in Dorchester which was started by people living in a scheme that accommodates low-income grandparents who are raising grandchildren. They partnered with a youth development organisation, a community development corporation and the Boston Architectural College to restore and renovate a community garden that had become neglected and dilapidated.

The resources for the whole project have come from a range of individual donors, giving both cash and in-kind donations. The Party has not yet attracted big corporate or public sector contributions, but at present the ambitions do not require this level of support. In fact, the Party suspended recruitment for new delegations once they reached the 70-member mark to ensure that it could both support the growing requirements and facilitate the community development aspect of the project.

Lisa and her colleagues like to accentuate the playfulness of their activities; the name is a humorous nod towards a significant event in the American War of Independence in the eighteenth century. They want to avoid the earnestness and seriousness of some sustainability initiatives and community cohesion projects by injecting a sense of fun into their work. If they simply stated that each pair of trees creates a new gathering place and opportunities for learning, exchange and participation while seeking to facilitate a lasting engagement with the issues of food access, health, environmental stewardship, biodiversity, public space and civic engagement, it would be accurate but too worthy for their liking.

The Boston Tree Party was not Lisa's first idea. A few years previously she founded the Urban Homesteaders' League (UHL), which is still active and is dedicated to helping people to understand and adopt sustainable urban living skills of all kinds, centred on the home. It is 'committed to re-imagining the good life as one that is meaningful, pleasurable, environmentally sustainable, and socially just' (UHL, 2010). Being a member of the League links you into talks, tours and demonstrations covering a range of topics, including ecological urban agriculture, urban livestock, food preparation and preservation, making your own skincare products and cleaning supplies, urban composting, basic carpentry, green retrofitting and fibre arts.

To understand how she came to be able to combine an affinity to natural processes, artistic symbolism and terrific organising skills requires a closer understanding of Lisa's background. She has a Master's degree in Fine Arts from the Boston Museum of Fine Arts and Tufts University in Boston. While majoring in art, she also took some environment courses as an elective. She grew up in the city of Washington, DC, so there were no obvious rural childhood experiences to explain her green interests. During her degree, she was heavily influenced by Rebecca Kneale Gould's (2005) book, *At Home in Nature*. She based her individual course project on the book which initially was an experiment, but then it turned into the League.

At first, there were just a few dozen people who met and discussed issues (mostly around food) at each other's houses. The group attracted quite a few 'gardening anarchists and off the grid people', but there were also ordinary people who just wanted to learn how to grow their own fruit and vegetables in the back garden. Lisa was well connected across the city and in nearby cities like New York. She quickly found herself in the role of event co-ordinator. In January 2010, she thought that the group was weighted a little too much towards better-off middle-class members and she sought to diversify the interests by contacting other like-minded organisations in the Boston area such as the Liveable Streets Alliance (for sustainable transport), the Green Justice Campaign (for home energy conservation and jobs for low-income communities) and Greenport (a community initiative inspired by James Kunstler and based in Cambridge, MA). Greenport resembled an early version of the Transition Town groups that were springing up in the UK and Ireland which based activities on self-sufficiency in the expectation of resource depletion and a reduction in the availability of fossil fuels.

As membership grew, there were more and larger themed meetings on issues such as energy co-operatives and permaculture. Lisa had the idea of reaching wider audiences by taking stalls at community fairs and farmers markets and handing out 'how to' flyers on subjects such as how to fit a rain barrel to a drainpipe, textile recycling, setting up honeybee hives, making pickles and eating seasonally. She realised that while the Homesteader agenda took in a wide range of issues, food was the most popular and unifying subject. She found that discussions with people about how to respond to climate change always felt laboured and depressing whereas a discussion about food was invariably positive.

This prompted Lisa to take an interest in a number of food-related social justice schemes such as the 'Bounty Bucks' scheme (run originally by The Food Project and later by the Boston Collaborative for Food and Fitness). The scheme was operated with the city authorities for low-income families who were in receipt of Supplemental Nutrition Assistance Programme vouchers (a scheme for people on state benefits). The scheme allowed recipients to spend the vouchers at local farmers markets instead of travelling to distant supermarkets. This was an alternative idea to overcome the food desert problems that have been tackled by fixed-point food retail stores in Pittsburgh, as described earlier in this chapter.

Lisa's ideas seemed to be tapping into some old concerns about the ability to cope in a contracting world, both in terms of a shrinking economy and a reduction in the availability of resources. They could be interpreted as a kind of Victory Garden for the twenty-first century. But there are also very modern influences at work here that that add notions of leadership and empowerment to take control of food, and a willingness to do something to arrest declining environmental conditions through the medium of food. Thus Lisa's efforts could be written off as a brilliant but isolated attempt to re-define sustainable living if it were not for an equally inspired project that has distinct parallels with her work on the other side of the Atlantic.

The British grow-your-own story

The first line of the Incredible Edible Todmorden (IET) website under 'what we do' reads 'we grow and campaign for local food'. Like Lisa's project, this is a deceptively simple description of a multilayered phenomenon. Their ambition is to make the town self-sufficient in food by 2018. While accurate, this does not nearly cover the work they do or the contribution this small group makes to a small town on the Lancashire/Yorkshire border. In fact, the longer you talk to the IET team, the more the conversation resembles one of the onions they are growing in the church graveyard. Apparently straightforward, the IET story covers issues as far-reaching as social cohesion, health, climate change and local economic independence. To understand the context behind the revolution in Todmorden requires a brief review of urban farming in Britain.

The story of household production of fruit and vegetables in Europe is very different to that in the USA, although there are still many urban projects that use food production in much the same way. However, because of the greater familiarity with 'allotment culture' in Europe, there are emerging movements originating from different directions that are harnessing this for wider purposes.

In the UK, land rented to grow food is known as an allotment. These are small strips of ground (typically rectangular in shape, encompassing about 250 square metres). They are usually found in groups of between 30 and 100 and bounded by a fence, typically although not exclusively in the vicinity of a municipal park or garden. The allotments are rented out to applicants and tenancies are renewed on an annual basis, provided the plot-holder abides by the rules. One of the strictest is that produce grown on the allotment must not be sold on as part of a commercial undertaking. The land is usually owned by a municipal or parish authority (some church authorities also own allotments sites) and governance is often delegated to an elected committee for self-management.

In England, the history of the urban allotment is often traced back to the establishment of the 'guinea gardens' of Birmingham in the 1850s. Prior to this, there was a long history of small areas of land tended by working people for personal consumption. Then the Industrial Revolution attracted large numbers of workers to move from the land into the growing towns and cities. These new factory workers looked for places where they could supplement their income by growing their own food and as a refuge from the often environmentally degraded areas in which they lived and worked. Throughout the Victorian era, Birmingham was a city known for being a hub for heavy industry and manufacturing. The guinea gardens were offered by a sympathetic land owner to those requesting small plots to grow fruit and vegetables. The idea influenced other municipalities and by 1873 there were almost 250,000 sites stretching across the whole country (Burchardt, 2002).

As in the USA, both of the twentieth-century World Wars resulted in a large amount of non-agricultural land being pressed into service to produce food. As a result, more of the population became exposed to, and skilled in, growing food. When the wars ended, much of the land reverted back to its original ownership, but this left a large number of people remaining interested in growing their own produce and this led to an increase in the demand for allotments. In 1949, the Allotments Advisory Body recommended that every local authority should set aside four acres per 1,000 head of population for the purpose of urban agriculture and this was enshrined in law in the Allotment Act of 1950. Since that time the interest in urban agriculture has fluctuated. The 1960s and 1970s saw a decline in allotment provision from over a million to around 500,000. However, a television situation comedy, *The Good Life*, which ran from 1975 to 1978, influenced popular culture in Britain and was responsible for a small revival in allotment farming. The popular programme featured a couple who wanted to be self-sufficient and converted their suburban house and garden into a smallholding, much to the irritation of their neighbours.

A further decline in interest in the 1980s tempted some local authorities to cash in their valuable land holdings and many were sold to house builders. After sinking to close to 250,000 sites at this time, there was a revival in the 1990s. The National Allotment Society reports that there are now over 330,000 allotment plots in the country, and demand is outstripping supply, exemplified by a waiting list of close to 100,000. Some have put the resurgence in interest down to a spate of food scares and reports of genetically modified foodstuffs entering the food chain. This may have motivated some people to ensure the provenance of their food by producing it themselves. Others may have been concerned about diminishing green spaces in towns and cities, influenced by campaigners working to ensure that allotments were being taken up and actively farmed and managed. A few more may have been inspired by the media focus on allotments, including a spate of television programmes about gardening, and thought they should join the trend to learn how to grow fruit and vegetables (Crouch, 2003).

While the fluctuation in the numbers of active food gardeners over the past 150 years is interesting, it is the changing demographics of modern allotment culture that made the biggest impact on British society. Throughout the Victorian era and right up until the 1980s a very high proportion of plot holders were male working people, often craftsmen, industrial workers, tradesmen, widowers and retirees. It was almost a certainty that new joiners would encounter a string of older men offering suggestions or pouring scorn on new crops or planting ideas. For some who did not fit the mould, this could be an intimidating atmosphere and one that tended to preserve the homogenous make-up of the typical allotment society. Today that image has been transformed and modern-day plot holders now resemble their surrounding communities. There are many more woman and children on British allotments now, and the ethnic mix has also widened to reflect the wider society. This has tended to produce a more supportive environment which in turn invites a more inclusive membership. However, with 26 million households in the country, allotment farming is still a minority pursuit although many more people have grown, and will continue to grow, food in their own back gardens.

Allotments in the UK have also been a popular way for social services and charities to integrate asylum seekers, refugees and other newly arrived immigrants into the community. In Liverpool, the charity Asylum Link (www.asylumlink.org.uk) has found land on allotment sites for dozens of asylum seekers and refugees for many years. In the USA, Michelle Obama brought attention to this aspect of community gardening when she toured the New Roots Community Farm in San Diego in 2010 (Ponsen, 2010). The city provides a four-hectare site for 80 refugees from countries including Somalia, Cambodia, Burma, Uganda, Congo, Kenya, Mexico, Vietnam and Guatemala to grow their own food.

The Incredible Edible revolution

Estelle and Mary are two of the central characters in the Incredible Edible story. While there are men on the team, it is clear when you talk to these committed and focused people that the organisation benefits from a woman's perspective. Mary was employed for many years as a community development worker for the local council (Calderdale). She regrets being made redundant in 2011 as a result of widespread public sector cuts suffered by many European countries in the wake of the economic slow-down. Her passion to this day is child health and protection (a clear link with Michelle Obama's motivation). When she was working for the council, she saw at first hand the problems that poverty can have on children from deprived backgrounds.

Mary has a very keen sense of where she is working and why she has committed herself to helping people to understand how to grow and cook fresh fruit and vegetables in a small town. Years of working with underprivileged people who may not have had adequate education has given her a distrust of others who were working in the same area. For example, she thinks the Transition Town groups have their heart in the right place but their language is all wrong. Talking about peak oil and permaculture will, in her opinion, fail to reach the great majority of people, particularly those who are in most need of understanding the main message. She is also very keen to point out that although the initiative she helped to set up is a grow–cook–eat initiative, it has no firm connection to either the organic movement or even vegetarianism. Mary says they need to start from where the people are and not from where they would like them to be.

Estelle is the creative in the team, working as an interior designer before she retired. In her late sixties (although you would never know it), she occasionally employs her age to disarming effect. When confronted with reactionary views harking back to better days, Estelle has been known to take off her hat, revealing a shock of white hair and rebutting some of the more obstructive rose-tinted arguments against their project. 'I remember the war too,' she countered to one man who thought that the new vegetable beds springing up in the town were nothing like the Victory Gardens of his youth. 'We are not imitating the past,' she tells him, 'we are helping people remember what we have forgotten.'

The Incredible Edible Todmorden (IET) story has much to do with the geography of the area. But equally it thrives because of the passion of the people who live there. Because of the steep-sided valleys there, some houses have front gardens at different levels to their front door. Mary decided to grow herbs on a patch that had previously supported a rose garden, but because the garden was not directly in front of the house, she found that some people were picking the leaves to flavour their meals. Instead of trying to protect her crop, she put a sign up, saying, 'Please pick what you need.' This act of generosity prompted a question: what would happen if the entire town was given over to the simple idea that everywhere you looked, there would be communal edible plantings? Because everyone would own the crop, there would be no need for fences. The only rules would be to preserve the concept of sharing and fairness. All you would need was the means to transport the food back home.

These ideas were underpinned by an experience that another founder member of the team had one day in London. Pam had gone to see a lecture by Professor Tim Lang, a food policy specialist and former advisor to the World Health Organization and numerous Parliamentary Committees. Pam's résumé matches her singular leadership skills. She was a Labour councillor for Calderdale and rose to become the Leader of the Council. She has served on many boards because of her expertise on countryside and regeneration issues, including Natural England, the regional Economic Development Agency and the Countryside Agency.

Pam had gone to hear Professor Lang talk about the growing crisis affecting global food chains. She came away deeply affected by his main message that difficult times are ahead. He highlighted the likelihood of increasing extreme weather events contributing to more frequent floods, droughts and heat waves. This, he explained, would make food more expensive or unobtainable and would interrupt communication and transport links that current food delivery chains relied upon to operate effectively.

On her trip back home, Pam realised that all this would threaten the viability of her home town unless the population could somehow act as one big self-support group. She reasoned that without kindness and selfless behaviours, the integrity of a small town like Todmorden could unravel when resources became scarce. People with low incomes would inevitably suffer more at first, but ultimately all of society would be damaged. She thought that if they could lead by example and do the small things well, then others would be encouraged to follow their lead.

Soon they were eying up council planters along roads and outside buildings that were covered in boring inedible greenery. Sometimes asking permission and sometimes not, they dug up the non-productive plants and put in herbs and later vegetables that were hardy and would grow all year round. People walking by would marvel at the leeks, cabbages and broccoli and children would ask what they were and how they tasted.

One of the most endearing terms associated with the IET movement became 'guerrilla planting', the surreptitious inserting of vegetables when the owner of the soil was not looking. After a number of high-profile visits, including one from Prince Charles, they have stopped needing to sneak around at night and have been invited to plant almost everywhere across the town. Consequently, they now call what they are doing 'propaganda planting'.

The ideas behind what they were doing started to attract funding opportunities and several orchards have been established and more are being planned. Public bodies that were initially wary of the guerrillas, particularly the local authority, were now lining up to get the IET treatment. The fire station, the railway station and the social landlord (Pennine Housing) were all happy to work with the IET team to find ways of involving their staff and the public in their radical ideas.

Many casual observers assumed that IET was a slightly eccentric healthy eating campaign and many journalists wrote the initiative up in those terms. But when you talk to Mary and Estelle, you hear terms like 'employment' and 'economic sustainability'. They know that jobs will make the town take the agenda seriously and they know that when the excitement of their work has finally died down, so will the grants and donations. The same realisation came to the Ashton Hayes and Sustainable Blacon teams. Consequently, IET is now working on a number of social enterprise ideas including a business to sell seedlings, another to make soap and produce honey, a 'food hub' at the local school, a working 'Incredible Farm', permaculture training and many others.

When asked about the now famous story about how they decided to plant up the police flower boxes with fruit and vegetables, they smile. They never tire of explaining that the police like to say that they are at the forefront of community relations but they never actually gave them permission to use their planters. It's more important to IET to talk about the outcomes of that work. Kids used to throw rocks at the police windows, but now they run in and shout 'I've been good' at the desk sergeant. Youths are now more likely to pose for photos next to the giant sweetcorn outside the station than rush past with hoods up. The relationship is so close that now IET have a deal that when the police confiscate the paraphernalia that goes with the illegal growth of cannabis plants (pots, compost, lights and liquid feed, etc.), it all gets donated to their projects.

Mutual benefit is another key issue for IET. In the local marketplace they've convinced stall holders to display blackboards that tell customers exactly where their products have come from, particularly when they originate from local growers and food producers. When horsemeat was found in beef products across Europe in 2013, a local abattoir in Todmorden was swept up in the controversy. News reporters descended on the town, asking local butchers if they were worried that trade would fall off as a result. Because IET had encouraged many of them to source their meat from local farms, they were able to explain that the scandal did not affect them as the problem stemmed from the international trade in meat products.

A local Polish doctor told them he used to grow strawberries back home and asked if it was possible for him to do the same in the cool Yorkshire climate. IET did better than that and planted them right outside his window at the health centre, delighting both him and his family. Other projects included planting up the tow path along the canal which was transformed into a linear farm, attracting mooring narrow boats. The grounds of the local home for the elderly have had the IET makeover, encouraging the inhabitants to come outside more often to work the beds or just enjoy the new edible surroundings.

When the town's supermarket had a sale of fruit trees, IET bought some and planted them in their own car park borders. The Boy Scout troop has been encouraged to do a new badge which says 'Grow, Cook, Eat' and one of the police station's old flower beds is dedicated to whatever the troop want to grow. They cook locally made sausages over a bonfire in the old Unitarian church gardens while listening to a talk about where food comes from and how to cook over an open fire. IET had to design and pay for the new badge, but if it is accepted, it will be available for Scout troops to tackle all over the world. While some at IET have reservations about the hierarchical nature of the Scouts, it is yet another way the group have found to disseminate their message in a subversive yet inclusive way.

IET is now very experienced at handling the media but they have never courted coverage or 'sold' a story. They (Estelle in particular) update the website on a regular basis, so when the local newspaper asked if they could fill a page a month, they accepted, knowing that there was ample material for the job. Cleverly, but wholly in keeping with their inclusive strategy, they have always tried to use the page to direct attention toward other groups as well as their own efforts, and this has won them many friends

The beauty of the IET model is that it is eminently stealable, which is exactly what the group wants. They noticed one day that the local theatre decided to replace the flowers in their planters with edible plants with no input from IET at all. Even the town drunks want to get involved and lurch out from under the canal bridge to offer help whenever they see the volunteers approach. But there are also times when the principle works in reverse. The logistical problems associated with the steep-sided valleys gave cause for concern as it means that there is limited flat space to store donations like the timber used to construct new planters and gardening supplies. When the deliveries arrive, there is no other choice but to pile up the materials in local car parks without any security or protection. In the whole time that material has been stored in this way, not a single item has been stolen.

The strategy is now infusing the normal life of the town. When Estelle shows off the range of planting in the graveyards, she explains with a beautifully controlled straight face that they were encouraged to do this because local people felt that it brought life to the area. When young lads were caught with their arms full of apples running headlong away from fruit trees, they immediately put the fruit down and looked shamefaced at those who stopped them. Shame turned to amazement when they were told to pick the fruit up again and go home with it because the crop was for everyone, and everyone is entitled to pick the produce when it's ready. Those boys have returned regularly ever since that incident to help out with the weeding and clearing of new planning beds. People are generally very pleased when they see their neighbours on TV, and they like being praised as one of those 'vegetable people' when they travel away from the town and tell others they are from Todmorden.

When asked to sum up their initiative in a few single words, they come out with 'trust' and 'passion', but particularly 'kindness'. That's a startling word when you are expecting to hear 'sustainability', 'healthy eating' and even 'community cohesion'. But it becomes clear when they start talking about their vision for the future that this word fits with the world-view of Incredible Edible members. They know that climate change will inevitably lead to energy shortages and problems with both the growing and the transportation of food. This is of course very similar to the views of the Transition Town groups, but whereas TT leaders talk in terms of science and geo-politics, IET people talk in terms of emotion and human interaction.

Because many of them have both come from and worked with people from lower-income backgrounds, they understand that it is this section of society that will be worst hit than others. They ask, 'When resources become scarce, who do you think is going to suffer?' But they also understand that people with more resources will not offer their help unless they experience equal amounts of care and kindness as their less privileged neighbours.

Unless there is a firm commitment and effort to bind the society of the town together in mutual respect and dependency, things will inevitable unravel when times get hard. In some ways it is incongruous that such a joyous movement is underpinned by such a dark vision of the future. Yet climate scientists been explaining for years that this is the outcome we can expect, and while many adaptation initiatives focus on planting new crops or ensuring that the vulnerable are protected from flood waters, IET is working on the human aspect to bind in trust and mutual dependency.

Forging a common bond between rich and poor is a daunting task that many societies have failed to achieve, but IET think that the gulf can be bridged by accentuating common links between human beings. Food is the one they consider to be the best lingua franca for a sustainable community in their town. Their strap line is 'If you eat, you are in.' Pam has been quoted as saying, 'Simply by using this language of food, we have opened up conversations, new ways of looking at space, new ways of working across our communities, new ways of bending existing investment. Believe me, I have seen the power of small actions and its awesome' (RSA, n.d.).

The entire ethos was put to the test over two separate weeks in the summer of 2012 when the town was hit by serious flooding after the UK's wettest summer in 100 years, and the wettest April to June ever. On 22 June, the town was inundated when the River Calder and the Rochdale Canal both overflowed their banks. The problem was caused after one month of rain fell in just 24 hours. Over 900 homes and dozens of businesses were affected and many residents had to move to upper floors as water filled ground floor rooms.

The floods showed up some unintended and not altogether welcome implications of the IET success in Todmorden. The water damage was severe enough to attract a visit from the Prime Minister David Cameron on 28 June. The first Mary knew about this was a telephone asking her to report to the Town Hall in the morning for 'an important visitor'. When she arrived, she was greeted by the chiefs of the police and the fire service and the mayor. She had to quietly ask why she was there and was told she was the 'community representative'.

When the council wants to organise something now, they call one of the IET activists because many feel the group is the face and heart of the town. Their Harvest Festivals were so well publicised, attended and covered in the press that that they are now effectively the social secretary for most things that take place in Todmorden, regardless of whether it is associated with their main mission. When asked why others are passed over for the organisational duties, the answer is usually, 'But you are the people who make things happen around here.'

Now, after the floods, IET members were named among the 'town champions'. This works both ways for IET. In some ways, it is the manifestation of their efforts to bring people out of their houses and away from their isolated lives. They do this to try to ensure that the largest number of people interact and get to know each other in anticipation of (even) grimmer things to come than severe flooding. But they also want people to be more proactive and not to rely on IET every time something needs to be done.

Some of what they have created has not always worked in the way they thought. When the second, more minor flash, i.e. surface, flooding occurred almost a month after the river and canal burst their banks, townsfolk donned high-visibility jackets and started directing traffic in a way that led to chaotic scenes until the rescue services arrived. The self-help Facebook page 'Calder Valley Flood Victims' put out a call for blankets and furniture which duly arrived by the truckload at the local college and then, because of the sheer volume, needed to be re-distributed, some of it to the dump. A few people who had been active with IET created a 'Food Angels' service which to some seemed a little over-dramatic. Some stranded residents were visited by so many would-be rescuers that they started to ask people to stand at their door to tell each new arrival that no additional help was needed. But even though some actions were counter-productive, IET said that the sense of pride of place which prompted people to help was a welcome change from earlier times when fewer people would have been prepared to make an effort for their neighbours.

One of the disappointments was that some of the collective organisation was directed at helping people to put in claims for government compensation for flood-damaged property. Mary said that there was a feeling of entitlement, that the whole town should be compensated for the floods. For her, this felt too much like they were falling back into a dependency culture and a reliance on paternalistic authorities. This ran counter to the self-help and self-sufficiency culture that IET has tried to engender. Finally, there was not much of a response from low-income estates, a reminder that the need to overcome economic hardship can be a tough competitor, even when your solution could ultimately help to solve this problem.

While some aspects of the floods did not go entirely according to plan, IET felt that these were happy problems in a place where previously community spirit had been hard to find. In a way, the flooding helped to underline their points about the difficulties the town can expect to experience with greater frequency because of climate change. They needed to be conscious of the hardship that flooded residents and businesses experienced and so did not express the point in those terms. The flooding had a similar effect on the people of West Yorkshire as Hurricane Katrina had on a section of the US population in the years after 2005. Then, as now in the UK, people are linking severe weather to global warming. While the IET message is and will continue to be grounded in food and food production, the weather prompts a conversation about why the world is changing. They say that the effect that the burning of fossil fuel has on local conditions is easier to make in the wake of a serious weather-related incident.

The IET team can see that audiences respond very well to the direct and engaging manner in which they put their story across. You can now see how this works by watching a TED talk that Pam gave to a very entertained audience (Warhurst, 2012). TED (standing for 'Technology, Entertainment and Design' with the strap line, 'Ideas Worth Spreading') was an obvious base from which to disseminate the IET. But the IET team also invite other speakers up to Todmorden and one night Tim Lang came to the town to present his ideas on food security to a PublicTod Talk session (based on the TED Talks format). Afterwards an angry local freemason approached Mary. Fearing the worst, she was surprised to hear that his anger was directed at the government for keeping these issues from the public and congratulated IET on the work they had done for the community.

You might expect a group like Incredible Edible Todmorden to seize on the opportunity to paint a brilliant picture of all the long-term goals they are planning to achieve. And yet, when this is put to Mary and Estelle, they look a little uneasy. They don't have a five-year plan or a set of objectives that they can show off as partly or mostly completed. This is not because they lack confidence in what they are doing; the opposite is true. But they admit that they have been so caught up in the whirlwind of interest in their ideas that they really have not had much time to consider the future. Some, like Pam, are clearly enjoying the opportunity to take the message to a wider audience. At the time of writing, she had been to Spain and Brazil, speaking at international conferences. Mary has been to Poland and will have made two different trips to the Netherlands in the same year. Estelle was fielding the third media approach from Taiwan in a couple of years, and groups from France, Italy and three different states in the USA, plus a phalanx of students from all over the world, regularly visit and place demands on their time.

Estelle points out that it is hard to turn people away because you never know who is going to come back later (sometimes years later) and contribute time and money to something that inspired them to change their lives. But Mary reflected that there are other times when they find themselves travelling miles to talk to a small number of people who were not their core audience. They are not entertainers although they are entertaining. They speak to effect change and they have learned that some audiences are not open to this.

And it is not just public speaking that they are reviewing now. Mary says that they are starting to have conversations about why they are devoting time to certain projects. A recent idea was to take on a major land asset in the middle of the town. They understood that it was a major financial commitment that could undermine or dominate their other projects. In earlier days they would have gone ahead anyway, but now they are asking more questions about the implications on their time and the most efficient way to continue to spread their message.

They are also getting better at generating income. At first it was important for them to be seen as a movement requiring little or no funding. The message was that anyone could be a propaganda planter and work up to uniting a community. But if listeners thought that this could only happen with a £1 million grant behind you, then it was a non-starter. Cash has become necessary to spend on travel, web development, materials and, in particular, apprenticeships so that some of the day-to-day tending and maintenance, and the conducting of tours can be taken on by the constant supply of talented, deserving young people who want to get involved.

So they now ask for appearance money and depending on the income levels of the organisation, they do charge a per head price for tours ('Vegetable Tourism', they call it). Their social enterprises are also now hiring and they hope to be in a position to generate many more jobs in the future. They could have tried to sell their idea to other towns and cities, but they opted for a 'free franchise' model instead. There are, at the last count, 37 Incredible Edible groups around the UK and many more in other countries. Some cultures have embraced the concept more strongly than the British. For example, there are now over 60 'Les Incroyables Comestibles en France', and the French show signs that there may be an IE group in every town and village before long.

To cope with all this burgeoning activity, IET is looking to establish the role of national co-ordinator for the whole UK network. This would allow each group to learn from everyone else and it could act as the first point of contact for the bewildering array of questions that come at them every day. In any one day Estelle will reply to questions like 'Where is my nearest IE group?'; 'When should you plant early fruiting raspberries?'; and 'Why won't my police station allow me to plant broccoli in their hanging baskets?'

Pam is working another channel through the RSA (Royal Society for the Encouragement of Arts, Manufactures and Commerce), a venerable group founded in 1754 and now known for its insights and interventions into British public policy. She is setting up projects that seek to go beyond communities and establish 'Incredible Centres of Learning' in universities and high schools to teach students to relate the way they live to the changing world around them. She is also thinking about creating a group of 'Incredible businesses' that organise sustainable supply chains and transform the main streets and local markets of the country.

Their strength may not lie in strategic thinking (yet) but they have an amazing ability to find common ground. Mary tells a story about being nominated for a 'Woman of the Year' award. She found herself sitting next to an army wife and, not owning a TV at the time, had no way of knowing that the woman had been on a programme about a servicemen's wives choir who went on to sing a Christmas Number 1 hit the previous year. The woman listened to Mary's story and commented that as she could not grow a thing, there was not much they could share. But Mary pointed out that the wives may not be able to do much to change the outcome of the conflict in Afghanistan, but they could form a local group and try to create something positive among themselves. Mary pointed out that was exactly what they were doing in Todmorden. The only difference was that the army wives were focused on war, while IET was focused on avoiding poverty and suffering as a result of resource depletion and climate change. Mary said they even found common cause with the Occupy Movement. Instead of Occupy Wall Street, they felt they were Occupy Small Town, challenging unsustainable living from within.

7 Has the green community come of age?

Understanding a complexified world

It is tempting after collecting a range of stories to try deconstructing them into the separate factors that made them successful. Policy analysts and (especially) academics like to examine the components of change and then build up a model based on the most effective parts of, in this case, each community initiative. The hope would be that policy-makers could roll out this new model in order to bring about lasting change to every other community that has not benefited from a green community group. After recording the rich diversity of backgrounds and views among the activists for this book and the contexts in which they operated, it occurred to me that this might not be a very fruitful pursuit. In a talk given as part of the 'As Yet Impossible' series at the University of Salford in England, on 13 November 2012, the MIT-based urban planner Michael Joroff said that it is always a mistake to try to simplify a world which is naturally complex. Homer-Dixon (2006) goes further, explaining that the complexity of the natural world has been exacerbated by multiple purpose-built interconnections in the human-constructed world. This is, he argues, a result of a misguided attempt by politicians and technocrats to fix our current unsustainable world by adding layers of technological and bureaucratic solutions.

Joroff says that any attempt to simplify the world only serves to soothe the minds of those who struggle to make sense of what we have become. It is not in any way constructive as a means of overcoming adversity, and could even create misunderstandings as interdependencies and synergies are overlooked in an attempt to boil the world down into its constituent parts. He thinks that problem-solvers should be working in the opposite direction and that societies need to undergo a process of 'complexification'. His made-up word is an attempt at 'getting back to reality'. This may be inconvenient for people who like to fix things and move on, but at least it forces decision-makers to confront the world as it is and not how they would like it to be. Those seeking to understand green community action in order to prescribe solutions for as yet unorganised neighbourhoods are only likely to take one lesson away after accepting this analysis: avoid cookie-cutter formats and concentrate on the factors that influence each community on their own merits.

This does not mean that we should not try to understand and mark the changes that are influencing people who are acting collectively for pro-environmental change right now. This could help to determine whether the environmental movement has indeed turned a corner, or whether current forms of organisation are simply moulding onto the current set of economic and environmental realities. A better understanding of the trends could have implications for public policy if this leads to new ways to facilitate localised groups to mobilise or simply to help to create the contexts in which they thrive.

Sources of inspiration: diversity in action

One of the striking things that comes out of the breadth of testimony given by those who are active in green community groups today is the diversity of backgrounds and motivations that have led them to their current pursuits. Quite a few said that they would not consider themselves as environmentalists. It is inevitable, given this diversity, that some will have been uncomfortable with the basket of beliefs and tactics that had previously characterised the movement. However, from their stories, it seems that most did feel their own life experience, beliefs and understanding of the movement gave them every right to campaign shoulder to shoulder with others who did call themselves environmentalists. This modesty in denying the title of environmentalist is not really justified, but could be explained by a weariness or suspicion of titles and labels. They just felt that they were acting to make their community better and were happy to leave it at that.

But it would not be accurate to simply attribute present-day green community activism to random acts of neighbourhood solidarity. Many of the stories of people active in Pittsburgh (Larimer, East Liberty and the Hill District) were very focused on the alleviation of deep and long-term poverty. Some sought to concentrate on environmental issues as a means to avert the continuation of this trend as the economy deteriorated. Those working in East Liberty's community development company or Hill House (the third-sector community organisation in the Hill District of Pittsburgh) saw how a focus on food and community gardens could act as a channel to remedy other problems, including poor health, poverty traps and the lack of investment for regeneration projects.

While it is not surprising to see a close connection between pro-environmental and social justice activity, there is still a perception that these causes are somehow in conflict. The tension between the environmental and the social justice movements has been somewhat of a distraction to those who have accepted that the social, environmental and economic aspects of society are and have always been inextricably linked. As Paul Hawken says:

It is only logical that environmentalists expect the social justice move-ment to get on the bus. But it is the other way around; the only way we are going to put out the fire is to get on the social justice bus and heal our wounds, because in the end, there is only one bus.

(2007: 190)

Fred at the Kingsley in Larimer and members of the original Incredible Edible group in Todmorden understood how damage to environmental con-ditions could or had actually hobbled the ability of the low-paid or those reliant on the state to rise out of poverty. While Fred concentrated on the condition of the built environment, Mary, Pam and Estelle came to see how food could be the starting point of a conversation about achieving a sustain-able community. Both Fred and the IET team (through different routes) had a clear vision of a worsening future if environmental trends were allowed to continue. This seemed to give them an urgency that was shared by some though not all of the other groups.

The food route was also a common theme in Lisa's work in Boston. But while she too was informed by a world-view of environmental disharmony through the courses she attended and the things she read, her thought process was inspired by an artist's perspective. Statement and metaphor in the public realm are not a common strand in the sometimes worthy, science-based world of the traditional environmentalist. It is hard to find a sense of fun in the agenda, perhaps understandably, given that the consequences of failure are economic collapse and mass extinction. And yet Lisa managed to work 'playfulness' in as a means of engagement. Much of the Incredible Edible programme also tries to steer away from the worthy and boring.

Fred, Mary, some of the Incredible Edible team and many of the Pittsburgh anti-frackers grew up in the area that they now seek to protect. It is perhaps an obvious assumption that people who have the strongest commitment to a neighbourhood have either grown up in the area or have lived there for a long time. But there did not seem to be any particular difference between those who had moved to their community recently or, like Ged and Chris, worked in a community but lived elsewhere. However, all did rely to some extent on finding recruits who had a firm desire to protect or enhance the area that they had come to associate with home.

The anti-frackers are similarly diverse in background, age and motivation. There were more expressions in this group of the anti-establishment sentiments that are often associated with the environmental movement. But not everyone came from a radical progressive background. John, from the Marcellus Protest, found that his anger was directed at the unethical corporate behaviour of gas exploration firms. He put this down to a career working for large companies. He was, if anything, even more disappointed than the ideologues because of his first-hand experience and his clear vision of how corporates should behave.

There were, of course, members of groups who were fire-brands, but many engaged in anti-fracking protest had led ordinary professional lives. Quite a few were over 60 and retired. They had served in sectors like health and education and could be forgiven for seeking out a gentler way to occupy their time like many of their peers. There were also a few reluctant protesters. These were people who felt compelled to stand in front of a TV camera but would rather have been somewhere else. Some had spent a lifetime objecting to injustice and easily added shale gas exploitation as the next issue to support. But others discovered the power in pitching an argument at local government or the media and had found that they liked feeling that they could change things, given the conviction and armed with a good argument. For these people, common struggle was invigorating and, in the case of the victories in the Pittsburgh area, thoroughly satisfying.

The activists in the community projects of Timperley, Blacon and Ashton Hayes had only geographic proximity in common. Garry and Alex had devoted their careers to environmental issues and are now motivated by thoughts of legacy and intergenerational issues. Like Fred and Mary, Ged was committed to helping the underprivileged and devoted himself to social justice issues. He also shared Lisa and Chris' experience in being inspired by studying environmental issues. Chris and Ged gained confidence in working with community members via social services programmes designed to help young families and the mentally ill. Alex, like Sue from RAFF (one of the Lancashire anti-fracking groups), is still working as an academic and Garry worked in communications and later as a consultant, mainly to the corporate sector. Like Alex and Sue, Martin and Peter in Vauban also held jobs in education and research.

This diversity in background and inspiration does not lend itself to a plan that targets any one sector or socio-economic type in order to find tomorrow's environmental leaders. But instead of viewing this as a weakness, perhaps the new emerging green community movement should view it as a strength, and even something to cultivate and preserve. Membership of some groups was purposefully left as inclusive as possible. In Todmorden, you only have to eat to qualify as a member of Incredible Edible. In Ashton Hayes, nobody will ever push you to join in, but you would be welcomed to contribute as much or as little as you want. This open door policy naturally invites a range of skills and views. The power of an inclusive movement comes into its own when there are complex problems to solve or there is a need to communicate with a range of people outside the group.

Ostrom (2012) understood that communities organising to preserve or change their areas were most successful when they contained a diverse range of active members. She saw that leaving problems unchecked led to unsustainable situations. She thought that it was important that no one discipline took charge of an agenda and that sustainable solutions could only be discovered when a range of different experiences came together. She warned against what she termed the 'panacea problem' when problem-solvers or policy-makers decided that there was a best way of doing things. While being clear that centralised or privatised solutions were often applied inappropriately, she cautioned against throwing them out en masse as occasionally they could be effective in certain circumstances. Similarly, a community solution was not always the best way forward. She pointed out that in the case studies she observed 'the governance systems that worked always fit well into their contexts. This is a clear indication that one type of solution does not fit all situations.'

In the academic world there has been a lot of discussion about combining different skills and expertise to solve new problems. This process is carried out in universities under the grand banners of interdisciplinary, cross-disciplinary and transdisciplinary thinking. In practice, this is even harder to do than it sounds. Often the language of the health practitioner, the criminologist, the ecologist and the engineer is so different in terms of both jargon and methodology that more time is taken up in translation than problem-solving. Joroff talks about this process in different, more accessible terms. He calls it convergence. MIT found that context is important in this process. He explained that some of the most interesting conversations and collaborations begin when people of different disciplines meet to play music together. He says that MIT has many chamber groups that play a wide range of musical genres because it's what people like to do when they relax. Talk in the breaks often gravitates to the problems they are wrestling with in their different knowledge worlds. They find that the different perspectives offered by others in their group often reveal solutions from unexpected directions.

The context of a green community group could well be performing the same function as the chamber orchestra. Here, people gather from solidarity positions to gain mutual support in the first instance. But once they get to know each other, they find that shared views help to clarify doubt and produce new ideas.

The question of leaders, leadership and inspiration

The evidence seems to support the value of diversity in green community groups, but there was another related, but separate, factor at work that came from the examples recorded in this book. Occasionally, one person embodies the collective understanding of a range of different disciplines. This was often due to the diversity of influences they experienced, sometimes over extended periods of their lives. This allowed them to occupy a leadership role, not necessarily because of their dynamic personalities, though many had this as well. Mostly it was because their diverse influences allowed then to articulate a vision that others could understand and follow.

There were many examples of people holding multiple influences and occupying leadership/inspiration roles in their organisations. Lisa combined arts and environmental science at degree level and then added organising and facilitation skills through experimentation. Garry combined communication and environmental science skills and added organisational and leadership abilities through working in and running a business. Pam had interests in the natural environment and regeneration, and added community and communication skills through her work in politics and other civic duties. Chris was influenced by an article about resource depletion and gained an insight into human behaviour and employee motivation by running a business in the mental health sector.

Perhaps it is not enough simply to be passionate about the place where you live to run a successful green community group, though this would seem to be a prerequisite. There also needs to be a few people who have ideas, drive and can articulate the whole of the problem to others. Mike Joroff calls these people 'outside insiders'. They are part of the organisation but they don't think like the rest of the organisation. He thinks that while having sufficient funding is important, it is not the key to effective change. Rather, the group depends on a few people who are prepared to try things out. They will be happy to take action and live with the risk that goes with this without really knowing the outcome. While this comes naturally to a few people, Joroff has seen how it is possible to create a culture that encourages more reticent innovators to venture into the unknown. MIT promises students that if their ideas keep within the rule of law and the institution, and do not harm the interests of others, they can produce installations (art, artefacts, pop-up stalls, etc.) and place them wherever they want for a short period of time. Occasionally the police come and take down the offending constructions but the university has been known to ask the police to put them back up again in support of the students. The culture recognises the outside insiders and nurtures them in the hope and expectation that their otherness will inspire those who witness their work.

The outside insiders description translates very well in a green community context. Here we have science, social empathy, art, behavioural science, communication skills and campaign strategy all rolled up in a few key individuals. There is also an acceptance that the world is complex. Nobody is trying to boil its problems down into universal solutions. It is a natural tendency for human beings to want to understand everything before they act, for fear of doing the wrong thing. This is particularly true in the corporate world where everything is usually required to be backed by an exhaustive evidence base. But out on the streets of Pittsburgh, Freiburg or Chester, there is no such requirement. It is odd therefore that many in the environmental movement have for so long tried to instigate action through the facts. Even those who were not inspired by *Gasland* or *An Inconvenient Truth* will recall the man setting fire to his water tap or Al Gore's heart-rending story about the premature death of his sister. But they fail to remember the phalanx of facts that accompanied these emotional images. Remember Ajzen and Fishbein's (1980) theory – that people need to care about the problem and know that their actions will be well regarded by others. This emotional side of the equation is equally important and many of the leaders of green community groups are able to transfer this to the rest of their activists and through them, hopefully, to the rest of the community.

Grass roots vs. top down

James Lovelock (the originator of the theory of Gaia) wrote that the environment movement 'should have been reluctant to found lobbies and political parties; both are concerned with people and their problems, and, like megaphones, they amplify demagogic voices of their leaders' (Lovelock, 2006). Clearly he was disdainful of the potential of top-down pressure to reverse environmental damage. There is no reason to doubt this on the basis of the unedifying performance of world leaders at world environment summits. For decades, they have serially failed to reach an agreement on, for example, the reduction of carbon from energy sources, the conservation of water or the protection of renewable resources from over-exploitation. Lovelock is not alone. His views are supported by many other influential authors and thinkers.

In his respected 'Plan B' series, Lester R. Brown sets out both the challenges and responses to the socio-environmental issues facing the world. In *Plan B 4.0* (Brown, 2009), he puts forward the three models of social change that could influence sustainability on a global scale. The first two models are what Brown terms 'Pearl Harbor' and the 'Berlin Wall'. The former requires a seismic change that virtually overnight transforms behaviour. The collapse of the Antarctic ice sheet or the ignition of the Amazonian rainforest could be examples of this. The 'Berlin Wall' is when pressure for change has built up for a while and then reaches a tipping point which has a similar spectacular effect on world opinion. The mass realisation that the burning of fossil fuel is harmful to global ecosystems leading to the rejection of coal, oil and gas by the consumers could be an example of this, if it came to pass. These would be effective, says Brown, but neither of them are likely to occur in the timeframe required to effect change.

This leaves the third and, in Brown's opinion, the most 'attractive' of the three models because it can work in a much shorter timeframe that the other two. He calls this the 'sandwich' model. This relies on 'strong grassroots interest in cutting carbon emissions and developing renewable sources of energy'. This grassroots movement then works with the interests of the governing authority, thus sandwiching the agenda between bottom-up and top-down pressure. Brown thinks he sees evidence that the environment movement is starting to effect change in the USA in an echo of the civil rights movement's gains in the 1960s. His advice to those who want to hasten change is to inform themselves of the issues, live more sustainable lives and lobby their elected representatives.

This would seem to be good advice if there was evidence that active green community groups put any faith in their elected officials. Certainly the anti-frackers in Pittsburgh have achieved some legislative victories at local government level, but the persistent efforts of the state (Pennsylvania) have not given confidence that anyone higher up is going to help. The food-based movements in both the USA and the UK have made use of some public monies to help their cause, but there is not much faith that this is going to be a central plank in federal policy-making, even with Michelle Obama's blessing. The activists in Vauban benefited from the wave of green enthusiasm from politicians at the start of the project. But some are suspicious about the motivation for this. If it was simply a shrewd capitalisation on the surge of anti-nuclear feeling, then the conviction could run out of political support if electoral winds start to blow the other way. Similarly, if the sustainability theme starts to cost more than it attracts in inward investment and tourist spend, then again there may be less enthusiasm from the city in the future. Many of the groups are looking for help from government, but they are also realistic and are not depending on support from this quarter. They accept that they are broadly on their own and need to concentrate on self-sufficiency rather than expending energy on talking to the higher echelons of the political world.

Ginsborg (2005: 171) explains that this is because modern-day democracies operate in an 'excessively separate sphere'. This has the effect, he says, of ensuring that there is 'no sense or culture of everyday politics, no mechanism by which ordinary lives are connected to extraordinary problems'.

Preparation in anticipation of deteriorating conditions

Some of the communities that agreed to be interviewed have invested heavily in fostering co-operation as a means to preserve community assets and resources. The fear is that when environmental and economic conditions deteriorate, this will limit access to resources like food and fuel. The social implications of this will be that the vulnerable and the less well-off will suffer first and disproportionately. Ultimately everyone will suffer as the fabric of society unravels. They argue that fostering co-operation and building trust prior to a crisis will make selfish behaviour more difficult when times get tough.

There are some who have tried to describe and understand this communal approach to the preservation of resources. The work of Elinor Ostrom is particularly relevant as she spent a considerable amount of time studying community behaviour. Professor Ostrom won the Nobel Prize in Economics in 2009, the first woman to hold that honour. Ostrom was a political scientist who had a life-long interest in understanding in 'how communities self-organise in response to various challenges' (Tarko, 2012). Since 2009 and the loss of confidence in market forces after the crash of 2008, economists have been compelled to ask questions about alternative systems to manage resources in a sustainable manner. In many ways, Ostrom's work could be seen as the continuation, in applied research, of Midgley's philosophical conclusion that co-operation is the best way to live in a sustainable society.

Policy-makers and economists who had previously held fast to a faith in market forces have become curious about Ostrom's ideas. Her work was directed toward social ecological systems and, in particular, she worked on solving the classic problem known as the 'tragedy of the commons' originally expressed by Hardin (1968). This describes how a commonly owned resource, exemplified by a grazing field, will become exhausted if it is used by competing farmers with equal access to the land. This is because each user will naturally act in their own interest until the resource is consumed or degraded to such an extent that it can no longer serve any or all of the interests without the need for a period of recovery.

Classical economists would prescribe one of two solutions to avert the tragedy. Either the common resource should be converted into private property (either by buy-out or parcelling into smaller units). Alternatively, it could be appropriated by the government and managed on behalf of the wider population. But Ostrom rejected this in her seminal work *Governing the Commons* (Ostrom, 1990). Instead she proposed a third option based on observed examples in different communities. In these examples, some members co-operated and together overcame the damaging effects of 'free riders' (those who benefit from other people's efforts but do not participate themselves). They did this by combining a number of factors which Ostrom described in one of her last public speeches (Institute of Economic Affairs, 2012).

In a sweeping review of her work, she said that successful communities managing what she termed 'common pool resources' had demonstrated four characteristics. They had established clear boundaries in terms of the duties of members, the issues under management and the geographical extent of their interest. They had congruence, a harmonious relationship with their locality and the environmental context in which they operated. They monitored conditions on a regular basis, allowing them to adapt to changing conditions, whether that was physical, political or economic. Finally, they had rules that were enforced with agreed conflict resolution systems. This ensured that collective decisions were discussed and when decisions were made, they benefited the majority of the members. Most also operated with high levels of trust within the group, had a large amount of autonomy within their area and invested in both leadership and social capital.

The governance systems in many of the groups I interviewed were well thought out, but resembled alliances and associations rather than corporate hierarchical units. The anti-frackers, in particular, were keen to keep their individuality as niche campaigners, but understood the importance of strength in numbers when this was required. The Boston Tree Party recruited 'delegates' or member groups from other organisations, who, with as much or as little facilitation as they wanted, were encouraged to adapt the initiative to their own purposes. The housing co-operative in Vauban was a highly democratised organisation that cared deeply about what the members wanted from their organisation, and the Incredible Edible teams have been very careful not to become the type of organisation that moves away from the community, even to the extent of rejecting offices or management structures.

There is an acceptance that this method of organising produces an unruly, looser type of group which can give present-day green community groups the appearance of a do-it-yourself movement. They hardly resemble the well-oiled campaign machines of the national or internationally organised environmental pressure groups. Many of the groups described in previous chapters were happy to campaign on dual and sometimes multiple levels as citizens, employees, members of single-interest or political associations and as part of a confederation of common interests. They all found governance systems that allowed them to function in a way that suited them and their causes. Instead of attempting to calm this riot of (dis)organisation, the diverse ecosystem of the green community should probably be accepted as the more natural way that pro-environment collectives will be run in the future.

While it is true that the today's green community groups may be fiercely independent, that does not mean that they are isolationist. Ostrom was also very aware that community organisations and individual actors did not operate in isolation and she developed an approach called Institutional Analysis and Development (IAD) (Ostrom, 1998). She identified a typical situation in which the way that the main protagonists engaged in the protection of resources played out within an 'action arena'. This is defined as a place where, for example, green community groups, the local authority and a regulator interact. The action arena can then be used as the context to predict the behaviour of each of the actors against a given proposition. Variables would include the physical conditions, the operating rules of the institutions and the attributes of the individuals and, collectively, of the green community group.

Ostrom's theories and her description of how the parties have interacted in the field are potentially helpful in understanding the changing landscape of green community activism. However, these need to be placed in context. Ostrom was ostensibly thinking and describing groups who were managing physical resources such as a fishery or a forest. Many of the groups in this book had a fairly clear geographic focus but were addressing global impacts, albeit on a local scale. This is a different context to Ostrom's original experiments, but she had also considered how her work could transfer to the issues being tackled by green community groups today.

At the end of her speech to the IEA, a member of the audience asked Ostrom how her ideas could be applied to an issue like climate change. She started by explaining that the tactics employed by the mainstream environment movement had not been successful in reducing the externalities (the results of greenhouse gas emission, for example) that are affecting families, local neighbourhoods, regions and cities. They have tried and failed to get sufficient numbers of locals to use less fossil fuel to lessen the effects of climate change. But she finds some hope in the enlightenment at local government level where 'over a thousand mayors in the US have signed an agreement to start working on various ways of reducing greenhouse gases in their cities'. She said that 'a thousand cities are quite different from just one'. The suggestion is that the scale of 'the commons' may be getting larger to encompass whole city regions, and if Ostrom's rules can be extended beyond the community scale, then more could be achieved though co-operation across wider populations. Ostrom ended her answer by saying, 'I am very nervous about just sitting around and waiting and making the argument that the rest of us can't do anything at all. So we need global action, but we can be taking action at multiple scales.' Ostrom's work is important because it helps us to understand green community activism thought the lens of governance. As soon as people agree to co-operate in a common cause, rules, about the way in which they operate, i.e., governance, are never far behind.

There are environmentalists who also have recognised the link between sustainability and the bonds that link community. Porritt (2005: 160) described two of the three success criteria underpinning sustainable natural systems as being self-organisation and diversity. But he recognised that these must be simultaneously 'shaped by mutual acceptance of the interdependent nature of each and every one of us, and by recognition of the fact that the purpose of society is to translate those mutual dependencies into effective relationships'. In their book about the importance of equal societies, Wilkinson and Pickett (2009) point out that the exact opposite is happening in many places. They say that people used to define themselves as part of the community to which they belonged. But the last few decades have seen people 'cast adrift in the anonymity of mass society'. This, they say, has the effect of undermining identity and self-confidence which in turn 'pushes people towards the refuge of self-affirming consumerism'.

It is possible that those who have enthusiastically embraced green community action have been attracted to their groups by the prospect of being an agent for change and in the process have rejected the isolation that the erosion of community naturally produces. In order to do this, leaders in the green community needed to have thought about the cultural context of their groups. For Incredible Edible in Todmorden, the context is kindness. For Lisa and the Boston Tree Party, it is stewardship. For Garry and Alex in Ashton Hayes, it is inter-generational responsibility and cooperation. Paul Hawken has observed a similar, less scientific and more emotional side to the emerging movement of the twenty-first century. He thinks that all groups organising for pro-environmental change share two principles. The first is that they would not expect to exert pressures on others that they would not wish to experience themselves. Second, they understand that all life is sacred. He questions whether these underlying values might be starting to 'permeate global society'.

The global/local link finally comes home

It is easy to see why the original think global, act local mantra did not appeal to those in government. How could you possibly effect change without some kind of over-reaching cross-boundary agreement? What difference would acting locally make if the fundamentals that make the world unsustainable were still in place?

The counter-argument is that global agreements are useless unless the people implementing them understand and agree that living and working in that way is beneficial and will make a difference. These arguments are not mutually exclusive and, as Lester Brown explained, the top-down/bottom-up pincer movement of change may well win out. But if there needs to be a choice, bottom-up will always be more powerful and long-lasting than top-down. If the majority of communities decide that sustainable change is the only way to defend their own and wider society, then there is not much that government or industry can do about it.

Before anyone gets too enthused with the move to local green community action, there is a qualification that needs to be made. It is possible, as we have seen in some of the accounts described earlier, to organise on a pro-environmental theme without reference to the wider world. Britain in Bloom has, as the Royal Horticultural Society pointed out, a value way beyond the beautification of towns, neighbourhoods and villages. But it is not necessarily going to change participants' world-view or even alter their habits and behaviours towards, for example, climate change.

Even when communities are seen to be organising to lower their carbon emissions like Ashton Hayes, the rate of change comes into question. This is the issue that Chris was wrestling with when challenged to export his ideas to a wider audience. Church (2012) is not so sure that the current local levels of action are sufficient. He says:

> Many groups are focusing on community energy – and helping create a much-needed low carbon infrastructure – but very few people would see this as more than a small part of the solution. We are clearly 'doing something' but is this really going to make a difference nationally or globally within the time scale when change is needed?

This is why it is so important to find evidence that new and emerging green community groups have understood the urgency required to address factors affecting global conditions and can relate them directly to the future of their own local communities. Previously, it was hard to find examples of this because of the disconnection between actions that had an intangible effect on global conditions and the specific impacts on people's lives. There are no cause and effect examples of people driving their cars too much leading to a severe flood affecting their house. More and more people need to understand the evidence, feel an emotional connection and then act upon it as if their lives depended on it. Up to now that has been a very hard sell.

The significance of the global/local link is important for gaining a wider awareness of the way unsustainable lifestyles impact on the wider environment. But the real breakthrough is when communities start to develop a sense of foreboding or anticipation that there are difficult times around the corner and that the ability to limit the effect of this is in their hands. This sense of anticipation fuels the urgency that has, at the very best, ebbed and flowed with the fortunes of the environmental movement to date. Marquand (2008: 347) agrees that the think globally, act locally slogan is a 'complex truism' that was more effective than the assertion that pollution did not respect international boundaries. This is because it places the power to effect change in the hands of local people. As Marquand states, 'Remote bodies like the United Nations or the European Union, or even the nation-state, could propose, but on a wide variety of environmental issues they could not dispose.' He goes on to say that on questions ranging from the recycling of waste to energy conservation, 'only a concerned and active citizenry working with strong local government could translate virtual aspirations into facts on the ground'.

The final element in the coming of age of the green community may be the belief, in greater numbers than ever before, that attempting to reduce (mitigate) or cope with (adapt) impending environmental and social change is worthwhile at a local level. There could be a range of motivations for this decision. It could be that some want to do something to protect the vulnerable. They may want to lead by example and start a movement so that other communities may be inspired to follow and therefore make a bigger difference. Others may want to send an unstoppable message to elected officials and the establishment that they need to acknowledge these new trends and change their policies or risk losing the support they crave. In many of the examples described in this book, all three reasons to act could be said to be at work in the same place.

The Transition Town movement says that the think global, act local advice is still relevant. The Transition Network website explains that:

> [People need to be] imagining what it might look like if every settlement had vibrant Transition initiatives; setting up food networks, energy companies, growing food everywhere and catalysing a new culture of social enterprise ... [because] the very notion of economic globalisation was only made possible by cheap liquid fossil fuels, and there is no adequate replacement for those on the scale we use them.
>
> (Transition Network, 2012b)

The advice continues with the assertion that 'the move towards more localised energy-efficient and productive living arrangements is not a choice; it is an inevitable direction for humanity' (ibid.).

Church (2012) concedes that green community activity creates a new infrastructure, draws people into doing things they may not have done on their own and 'bears witness', showing how others in the neighbourhood are saving energy, thinking about preserving resources and showing that 'there are people here and now who care enough to act on this global issue'. Others have found that there is more to green community engagement than a few greenhouse gas emission statistics. When the Evaluation Report for the LCCC scheme was carried out, it looked at a range of benefits beyond the energy-related achievements. The report (DECC, 2012b) listed the achievements such as 'well-being, awareness of the relationship between behaviour and environmental impacts, community empowerment and social inclusion'. The conclusions state that 'these social benefits are recognised as being important. The extent to which [they] are realised, however, largely depends on the process of decision-making, participation and implementation, and the model of ownership employed' (ibid.). In other words, the way that communities govern themselves and the inclusivity they engender are crucial to judging whether they have been successful.

Like Ostrom, Church thinks that communities need to become part of a wider, multi-sector, multi-agency effort to overcome the threat of climate change. His recipe is, with authorities and businesses, to jointly create a long-term vision for their area with underpinning evidence about how far the community needs to go before the job is done. He thinks there should be a strategy for both mitigation and adaptation, and regular reporting on progress. There should also be a constant advisory source to help people act on the strategy, preferably working out of a centre or 'hub'.

There is not much wrong with this prescription if communities have the time and interest to produce and maintain it. The evidence from this book is that many communities have had enough of plans, policies and politicians underperforming on their behalf. Ashton Hayes banned politicians from speaking at their meetings. The anti-frackers have grave doubts about the help their communities can expect from elected officials. There were parts of the Vauban community who were mistrustful of the motives behind some political support for their project. As ever, there are no blanket rules covering the conduct or beliefs of the green community movement, but even if a sizeable minority rejected the advances of a strategic approach from their authorities, it would probably not be a very effective plan.

E.O. Wilson (2002) said that if environmentalism had taught us anything, it was that

> a change of heart occurs when people look beyond themselves to others, and then to the rest of life. It is strengthened when they also expand their view of landscape from parish to nation and beyond, and their sweep of time from their own life spans to multiple generations and finally to the extended future history of humankind.

There are perhaps two main lessons for policy-makers and strategists to consider as a result of the evidence from this and other accounts of green community action. The first is that, where people are sensing an impending threat from deteriorating environmental condition, they may be looking more towards their community rather than government for comfort and security. If this indicates a growing trend, then both authorities and the wider environment movement need to take community action more seriously as this is where the motivation to take pro-environmental action is likely to start. Light (2010) makes this same point when he says that environmentalists need to move on from a focus on wilderness because 'as the importance of place is tied to the stories we can tell about it, then our understanding of the importance of place changes with new experiences'.

The second point concerns the time it is going to take for the majority of the population to get to the level of activism described in this book. Clearly, communities organising on a scale that will make a difference to their area are still in the minority. While there is evidence that (individually) there is concern about the implications of an unsustainable world, there is not enough collective action to change the predicted impacts in the timeframe required. While we know the consensus of many behavioural scientists is that it is hard to change people's minds, policy-makers can do much more to change the contexts within which people decide how to behave. Investment in the capacity of communities to help themselves and a focus on various ways to incentivise people to consider alternative ways of living and co-operating are just two ways that authorities could help to shape community contexts.

Paul Hawken is optimistic for the future. He says that the thinking that informs the movement will 'soon suffuse most of our institutions, but before then, it will change a sufficient number of people so as to begin the reversal of centuries of frenzied self-destructive behaviour' (Hawken, 2007: 189). Others, like James Lovelock, suspect that we may have passed the time when we can stop the destructive forces that are becoming more apparent year by year. Time will tell which of these outlooks is right, but one thing is certain; if resources continue to be used up at the current rate of consumption, then there does not seem to be much hope.

The hope lies in people at a local level refusing to wait to be rescued. They should be mindful of global trends and believe that their efforts will make a difference. These are not the kind of inclinations that many people naturally possess, but there is evidence that they can be learned and acquired from observing the activity that is going on around them. That willingness to confront the status quo and to learn better ways of living cannot be motivated by ministerial pronouncements or public service bulletins. They have to come from trusted members of the same community who can lead by example, be questioned for guidance, be looked upon for leadership and be on hand for encouragement. As we have seen from the accounts in this book, this process is happening in certain places, but other communities may need encouragement to start this process. If local and national government have any role at all in this process, it is to invest in the capacity of communities to be in control of their own destinies. This could include new and better places to meet, improved and affordable communications like fast broadband, the support to help neighbourhoods to organise into energy or housing co-operatives and to acquire land and buildings through vehicles like community land trusts. Beyond this, the people behind the emerging green community movement have shown that they are quite capable of organising and building sustainable places all by themselves. In this sense, the green community has truly come of age.

Bibliography

Agyeman, J. and Angus, B. (2003) 'The Role of Civic Environmentalism in the Pursuit of Sustainable Communities', *Journal of Environmental Planning and Management*, 46(3): 345–363.

Ajzen, I. and Fishbein, M. (1980) *Understanding Attitudes and Predicting Social Behavior*, Englewood Cliffs, NJ: Prentice Hall.

Bichard, E. and Cooper, C.L. (2008) *Positively Responsible: How Business Can Save the Planet*, Oxford: Butterworth-Heinemann.

Bichard, E. and Kazmierczak, A. (2009) *Resilient Homes: Reward-Based Methods to Motivate Householders to Address Dangerous Climate Change*, Salford: University of Salford. Available at: usir.salford.ac.uk/11276/5/report_FINAL_160909-2.pdf.

Bichard, E. and Thurairajah, N. (2011) *Resilient Homes (Phase 2): The Timperley Green Homes Trial on Methods to Motivate Homeowners to Address Property Level Effects of Climate Change*, report to the Environment Agency (of England and Wales) and Trafford Borough Council, University of Salford, available at: http://usir.salford.ac.uk/18381/1/Timperley_Green_Home_Final_whole_report_06.10.2011.pdf.

Breyer, F., Richter, M., Kern, N., Lang, F., Halter, M., Horstkötter, N., Zinthäfner, P. and Ahuis, M. (2011) *Green City Freiburg: Approaches to Sustainability*, Freiburg: Wirtschaft Touristik und Messe GmbH & Co. KG.

Brown, L.R. (2009) *Plan B 4.0: Mobilising to Save Civilisation*, New York: W.W. Norton.

Burchardt, J. (2002) *The Allotment Movement in England, 1793–1873*, London: Royal Historical Society.

Chestney, N. (2013) 'Britain Plans Tax Breaks for Shale Gas Investment', Reuters (UK edition), 19 July, available at: http://uk.reuters.com/article/2013/07/19/uk-britain-shale-idUKBRE96H1H320130719 (accessed 10 August 2013).

China Daily (2012) 'Sinopec Starts Work on Shale Gas Production Demo Area', available at: http://europe.chinadaily.com.cn/business/2012-10/25/content_15846822.htm (accessed 21 February 2013).

Church, C. (2012) 'Local Action on Climate Change: Not "Fit For Purpose" – Time for a Rethink and a Renaissance?', 10 September, available at: www.communityenvironment.org.uk/chris-blog/local-action-on-climate-change-not-fit-for-purpose-time-for-a-rethink-and-a-renaissance/ (accessed 5 January 2013).

Cialdini, R. (2004) *Influence: Science and Practice*, Boston: Allyn & Bacon.

——(2007) 'Basic Social Influence Is Underestimated', *Psychological Inquiry*, 16(4): 158–161.

COGCC (n.d.) 'Statement from the Colorado Oil and Gas Conservation Commission on Claims Made in the Documentary "Gasland"', available at: http://cogcc.state.co.us/library/GASLAND%20DOC.pdf (accessed 20 December 2012).

Committee on Energy and Commerce (2011) 'Chemicals Used in Hydraulic Fracturing', United States House of Representatives Committee on Energy and Commerce, Minority Staff, April 2011, available at: http://democrats.energycommerce.house.gov/sites/default/files/documents/Hydraulic%20Fracturing%20Report%204.18.11.pdf (accessed 12 December 2012).

Confino, J. (2012) 'Rio+20: Tim Jackson on How Fear Led World Leaders to Betray Green Economy', *Guardian*, 25 June, available at: www.guardian.co.uk/sustainable-business/rio-20-tim-jackson-leaders-green-economy (accessed 13 January 2013).

Coyne, J. (2012) 'Hill District Shop 'n Save to Be Constructed Soon', *Pittsburgh Business News*, 9 November, available at: www.bizjournals.com/pittsburgh/news/2012/11/08/hill-district-shop-n-save-to-be.html?page=all (accessed 2 February 2013).

Crouch, D. (2003) *The Art of Allotments: Culture and Cultivation*, Nottingham: Five Leaves.

DECC (2012a) 'Government Response to Royal Academy of Engineering and Royal Society Report on "Shale Gas Extraction in the UK: A Review of Hydraulic Fracturing"', Version: Final A04 – 10 December 2012, available at: www.gov.uk/government/uploads/system/uploads/attachment_data/file/49541/7269-government-response-sg-report-.pdf (accessed 30 January 2013).

——(2012b) *Low Carbon Community Challenge: Evaluation Report*, July, available at: www.gov.uk/government/uploads/system/uploads/attachment_data/file/48458/5788-low-carbon-communities-challenge-evaluation-report.pdf (accessed 21 November 2012).

Detwiler, C. (2011) 'Jobs and Community Benefits: Deconstructing Gas Industry "Messaging"', unpublished report.

Devine-Wright, P. (2012) 'Explaining "NIMBY" Objections to a Power Line: The Role of Personal, Place Attachment and Project-Related Factors', *Environment and Behaviour*, doi: 10.1177/0013916512440435 Environment and Behaviour, *April 17, 2012 0013916512440435*.

Dominiczak, P. (2013) 'Frack the "Desolate" North East, Says Tory Peer (Who Lives in the South)', *Telegraph*, 30 July, available at: http://www.telegraph.co.uk/news/politics/10211109/North-East-is-desolate-says-George-Osbornes-Government-adviser-father-in-law.html (accessed 10 August 2013).

Doyle, A. (2013) 'New Group Seeks to Save Near-Lawless Oceans from Over-Fishing', Reuters, 10 February, available at: www.reuters.com/article/2013/02/11/environment-oceans-idUSL5N0B8BRU20130211 (accessed 11 February 2013).

ELDI (2010) *East Liberty Community Plan: Many Voices Driving Neighborhood*, Pittsburgh, PA: East Liberty Development Inc.

Elkington, J. (1997) *Cannibals with Forks: The Triple Bottom Line of 21st Century Business*, Oxford: Capstone Publishing.

EPA (2012) 'Methane and Nitrous Oxide Emissions from Natural Sources', Office of Atmospheric Programs (6207J) EPA 430-R-10-001, Washington, DC: EPA, available at: www.epa.gov/methane/pdfs/Methane-and-Nitrous-Oxide-Emissions-From-Natural-Sources.pdf (accessed 12 January 2013).

Ferman, B. (1996) *Challenging the Growth Machine: Neighborhood Politics in Chicago and Pittsburgh*, Lawrence, KS: University Press of Kansas.

Ferris, D. (2002) 'Promoting Community Building Through Collaborative Environmental Justice Legal Strategies and Funding Approaches', paper presented at

Second National People of Color Environmental Leadership Summit: Summit II, Resource Paper Series, Washington, DC, 23 October.

Forum Vauban English (n.d.) 'Introduction to the Vauban District, Freiburg', available at: www.vauban.de/info/abstract.html (accessed 30 September 2012).

Ginsborg, A. (2005) *The Politics of Everyday Life: Making Choices, Changing Lives*, New Haven, CT: Yale University Press.

Goldenberg, S. (2009) 'Energy and Emissions Top Obama's Green Task List', *Guardian*, 19 January, available at: www.guardian.co.uk/environment/2009/jan/19/obama-environment (accessed 30 January 2013).

Goldsmith, E., Allen, R., Allaby, M., Divoll, J. and Lawrence, S. (1972) 'A Blueprint for Survival', *The Ecologist*, 2(1), special issue.

Gould, R.G. (2005) *At Home in Nature: Modern Homesteading and Spiritual Practice in America*, Berkeley, CA: University of California Press.

Gross, L. (2011) 'Boston Tree Party Inauguration', available at: www.bostontreeparty.org/join/inauguration/ (accessed 13 January 2013).

Halpern, D. (2005) *Social Capital*, Cambridge: Polity Press.

Halpern, D. and Bates, C. (2004) *Personal Responsibility and Changing Behaviour: The State of Knowledge and Its Implications for Public Policy*, London: Cabinet Office, Prime Minister's Strategy Unit.

Hansard (1994) 'Business of the House, 21 April 1994', Vol. 241 cc1039–52, available at: http://hansard.millbanksystems.com/commons/1994/apr/21/business-of-the-house. (accessed 29 December 2012).

Haq, G. and Paul, A. (2012) *'Environmentalism Since 1945*, London: Routledge.

Hardin, G. (1968) 'The Tragedy of the Commons', *Science*, NS, 162(3859): 1243–1248.

Haszeldine, S. (2011) 'Shale Gas, NW England Earthquakes, and UK Regulation', briefing note for the Department of Energy and Climate Change, available at:https://www.gov.uk/government/uploads/system/uploads/attachment_data/file/66758/5223-shale-gas-nw-england-earthquakes-briefing.pdf (accessed 20 January 2013).

Hawken, P. (2007) *Blessed Unrest: How the Largest Movement in the World Came into Being and Why No One Saw It Coming*, New York: Viking Penguin.

HFFI (2010) 'Healthy Food Financing Initiative: Implementation Plan', May, available at: www.ams.usda.gov/AMSv1.0/getfile?dDocName=STELPRDC5085689 (accessed 22 February 2013).

Hoggett, P. (2013) 'Climate Change in a Perverse Culture', in S. Weintrobe (ed.) *Engaging with Climate Change: Psychoanalytic and Interdisciplinary Perspectives*, London: Routledge.

Homer-Dixon, T. (2006) *The Upside of Down: Catastrophe, Creativity and the Renewal of Civilisation*, Washington, DC: Island Press.

Hopkins, R. (2008) *The Transition Handbook: From Oil Dependency to Local Resilience*, Vermont: Chelsea Green Publishing.

Hoppner, C. and Whitmarsh, L. (2011) 'Public Engagement in Climate Action: Policy and Public Expectations', in L. Whitmarsh, S. O'Neil, and I. Lorenzoni (eds) *Engaging the Public with Climate Change*, London: Earthscan, pp. 47–65.

Howarth, R.W., Santoro, R. and Ingraffea, A. (2011) 'Methane and the Greenhouse-Gas Footprint of Natural Gas from Shale Formations', *Climatic Change Letters*, 105: 5, available at: www.sustainablefuture.cornell.edu/news/attachments/Howarth-EtAl-2011.pdf (accessed 12 January 2013).

IEA (2012) *Golden Rules for a Golden Age of Gas: A World Energy Outlook, Special Report on Unconventional Gas*, Paris: International Energy Agency, available at: www.worldenergyoutlook.org/goldenrules/#d.en.27023 (accessed 15 December 2012).

Institute of Economic Affairs (2012) 'Annual IEA Hayek Memorial Lecture', 29 March, available at: www.iea.org.uk/events/annual-iea-hayek-memorial-lecture-1 (accessed 12 January 2013).

ITV (2013) 'Prince Charles: First Grandchild Reaffirms Green Beliefs', 6 January, available at: www.itv.com/news/2013-01-06/prince-charles-first-grandchild-reaffirms-green-beliefs/ (accessed 17 January 2013).

Jackson, T. (2009) *Prosperity Without Growth?* Report for the Sustainable Development Commission, London: Earthscan.

Jacobs, M. (1999) *Environmental Modernisation: The New Labour Agenda*, Fabian pamphlet no. 391, London: The Fabian Society.

John, P., Smith, G. and Stoker, G. (2009) 'Nudge Nudge, Think Think: Two Strategies for Changing Civic Behaviour', *The Political Quarterly*, 80(3): 317–456.

Kelly, J. (2012) 'Growing Civic Fruit: A Documentary Film about the Boston Tree Party', available at: www.homegrown.org/video/growing-civic-fruit-a-documentary-film-about-the-boston-tree?xg_source=activity (accessed 13 January 2013).

Ladner, P. (2011) *The Urban Food Revolution: Changing the Way We Feed Cities*, Gabriola Island, Canada: New Society Publishers.

Lawson, L.J. (2005) *City Bountiful: A Century of Community Gardening in America*, Berkeley, CA: University of California Press.

Lertzman, R.A. (2013) 'The Myth of Apathy', in S. Weintrobe (ed.) *Engaging with Climate Change: Psychoanalytic and Interdisciplinary Perspectives*, London: Routledge.

Light, A. (2010) 'The Moral Journey of Environmentalism', in S.A. Moore, *Pragmatic Sustainability: Theoretical and Practical Tools*, London: Routledge.

Lorenzoni, I., Nicholson-Cole, S. and Whitmarsh, L. (2007) 'Barriers Perceived to Engaging with Climate Change among the UK Public and their Policy Implications', *Global Environmental Change*, 17: 445–459.

Lovelock, J. (2006) *The Revenge of Gaia: Why the Earth Is Fighting Back and How We Can Still Save Humanity*, London: Penguin Books.

Marquand, D. (2008) *Britain Since 1918: The Strange Career of British Democracy*, London: Orion Books.

McCarthy, J., Canziani, O., Leary, N., Dokken, D. and White, K. (eds) (2001) 'Climate Change 2001: Impacts, Adaptation, and Vulnerability', contribution of Working Group II to the *Third Assessment Report of the Intergovernmental Panel on Climate Change*, Cambridge: Cambridge University Press.

Midgley, D. (ed.) (2005) *The Essential Mary Midgley*, London: Routledge.

Morello-Frosch, R., Pastor, M., Sadd, J. and Shonkoff, S. (2009) *The Climate Gap: Inequalities in How Climate Change Hurts Americans and How to Close the Gap*, available at: dornsife.usc.edu/pere/documents/The_Climate_Gap_Full_Report_FINAL.pdf.

Navarro, M. (2012a) 'New Jersey Senate Bans Treatment of Fracking Waste', *New York Times*, 25 June, available at: http://green.blogs.nytimes.com/2012/06/25 new-jersey-senate-bans-treatment-of-fracking-waste/ (accessed 14 November 2012).

——(2012b) 'Court Rejects a Ban on Local Fracking Limits', *New York Times*, 26 July, available at: http://green.blogs.nytimes.com/2012/07/26/court-rejects-a-ban-on-local-fracking-limits/ (accessed 20 November 2012).

Obama, M. (2012) *American Grown: The Story of the White House Kitchen Garden and Gardens Across America*, New York: Crown Publishers.

Ostrom, E. (1990) *Governing the Commons: The Evolution of Institutions for Collective Action*, Cambridge: Cambridge University Press.

——(1998) 'The Institutional Analysis and Development Approach', in E.T. Loehman and D.M. Kilgour (eds) *Designing Institutions for Environmental and Resource Management*, Cheltenham: Edward Elgar Publishing.

——(2012) *The Future of the Commons: Beyond Market Failure and Government Regulation*, London: The Institute for Economic Affairs.

Paige, J. (2011) 'Blackpool Earthquake Tremors May Have Been Caused by Gas Drilling', *Guardian*, 11 June, available at: www.guardian.co.uk/uk/2011/jun/01/blackpool-earthquake-tremors-gas-drilling (accessed 19 December 2012).

PBPC (2011) 'Statement on Gas Industry-Financed Report on Marcellus Shale's Economic Impact', report by the Pennsylvania Budget and Policy Centre, 20 July, available at: http://pennbpc.org/statement-gas-industry-financed-report-marcellus-shales-economic-impact-1 (accessed 22 December 2012).

Platt, R. (2011) *Green Streets, Strong Communities*, available at: www.ippr.org/images/media/files/publication/2011/07/green-streets-strong-communities_July2011_7703.pdf (accessed 29 January 2013).

Ponsen, A. (2010) 'Refugees Plant New Roots at Community Farm', *International Rescue Committee*, 15 April, available at: www.rescue.org/news/refugees-plant-new-roots-community-farm-7351 (accessed 13 January 2013).

Porritt, J. (2005) *Capitalism As If the World Mattered*, London: Earthscan.

——(2009) 'My Debt to Teddy Goldsmith', 11 September, available at: www.jonathonporritt.com/blog/my-debt-teddy-goldsmith (accessed 3 December 2012).

Purvis, A. (2008) 'Is This the Greenest City in the World?', *Observer*, 23 March, available at: www.guardian.co.uk/environment/2008/mar/23/freiburg.germany.greenest.city (accessed 29 November 2012).

Redwood, C. and Young-Laing, B. (2012) 'Organising for Economic Justice: A Model', in A. Emejulu (ed.) *Community Development in the Steel City: Democracy Justice and Power in Pittsburgh*, Edinburgh: Community Development Journal Ltd.

RHS (2011) *Britain in Bloom: Transforming Local Communities*, London: Royal Horticultural Society.

RSA (n.d.) 'The Big Idea: The Power of Small Actions on a Community', available at: www.thersa.org/fellowship/news/incredible-edible (accessed 13 January 2013).

Sanderson, K., Gertler, M., Martz, D. and Mahabir, R. (2005) *Farmers Markets in North America: A Literature Review*, Saskatchewan: Community-University Institute for Social Research (CUISR), University of Saskatchewan.

Secrett, C. (2011) 'An Open Letter to the Green Movement', 21 June, available at: www.guardian.co.uk/environment/2011/jun/21/charles-secrett-open-letter-activists (accessed 26 January 2011).

Schultz, P.W., Nolan, J., Cialdini, R., Goldstein, N. and Griskevicius, V. (2007) 'The Constructive, Destructive, and Reconstructive Power of Social Norms', *Psychological Science*, 18: 429–434.

Schultz, P.W. and Tabanico, J. (2008) 'Community-Based Social Marketing and Behavior Change', in A. Cabaniss (ed.) *Handbook on Household Hazardous Waste*, Lanham, MD: Government Institutes Press, pp. 133–157.

Scott, F. (2010) *New Times, New Connections*, London: Green Alliance.

Shackford, S. (2011) 'Natural Gas from Fracking Could Be "Dirtier" Than Coal, Cornell Professors Find', 11 April, available at: www.news.cornell.edu/stories/April11/GasDrillingDirtier.html (accessed 14 September 2012).

Shadbush (2013) 'About the Shadbush Environmental Justice Collective', available at: http://shadbushcollective.org/about/ (accessed 21 February 2013).

Shellenberger, M. and Nordhaus, T. (2004) 'The Death of Environmentalism', available at: www.grist.org/news/maindish/2005/01/13/doe-reprint/ (accessed 23 January 2013).

Smith, J.B., Schneider, S.H., Oppenheimer, M., Yohe, G.W., Hare, W., Mastrandrea, M.D. and Van Ypersele, J.P. (2009) 'Assessing Dangerous Climate Change Through an Update of the Intergovernmental Panel on Climate Change (IPCC) "Reasons for Concern"', *Proceedings of the National Academy of Sciences*, 106(11): 4133–4137.

Stern, N. (2006) *The Economics of Climate Change* (The Stern Review), London: HM Treasury.

Stern, P.C. (2009) 'How Psychology Can Contribute to Meeting the Challenge of Climate Change', address to the Psychology and Climate Change Policy Conference, RSA, London, 27 October.

Stoker, S.E. and Robert, C. (1996) 'Hill District Community Plan', 29 May, available at: www.ucsur.pitt.edu/files/nrep/other/HillDistrictCommuntyPlan_May291996.pdf (accessed 11 October 2012).

Sustainable Consumption Roundtable (2006) *I Will If You Will: Towards Sustainable Consumption*, available at: www.sd-commission.org.uk/publications/downloads/I_Will_If_You_Will.pdf (accessed 12 November 2012).

Tarko, V. (2012) 'Elinor Ostrom's Life and Work', in *The Future of the Commons*, London: The Institute of Economic Affairs in Association with Profile Books Ltd.

Transition Network (2012a) 'What Is a Transition Initiative?', available at: www.transitionnetwork.org/support/what-transition-initiative (accessed 8 January 2013).

——(2012b) 'Ingredients', available at: www.transitionnetwork.org/ingredients (accessed 13 January 2013).

UHL (2010) 'About the Urban Homesteaders' League', available at: www.meetup.com/Urban-Homesteaders-League/ (accessed 13 January 2013).

UN News Centre (2008) 'Secretary-General calls for "Green New Deal" at UN Climate Change Talks', *UN News Centre*, 11 December, available at: www.un.org/news (accessed 21 January 2013).

UT (2012) 'The University of Texas at Austin Energy Poll', Fall 2012, available at: www.utenergypoll.com/explore/past-charts/ (accessed 12 October 2012).

Warhurst, P. (2012) 'How We Can Eat Our Landscapes', TEDSalon, London, Spring 2012 (filmed in May 2012 and posted in August 2012), available at: www.ted.com/talks/pam_warhurst_how_we_can_eat_our_landscapes.html (accessed 13 January 2013).

Warner, N.R., Jackson, R.B., Darrah, T.H., Osborn, S.G., Down, A., Zhao, Z., White, A. and Vengosh, A. (2012) 'Geochemical Evidence for Possible Natural Migration of Marcellus Formation Brine to Shallow Aquifers in Pennsylvania', *PNAS*, 109 (30): 11961–11966.

Weber, C.L. and Matthews, S.H. (2008) 'Food-Miles and the Relative Climate Impacts of Food Choices in the United States', *Environmental Science and Technology*, 42 (10): 3508–3513.

Weintrobe, S. (ed.) (2013) *Engaging with Climate Change: Psychoanalytic and Interdisciplinary Perspectives*, London: Routledge.

WFM (2013) 'Community Giving', available at: www.wholefoodsmarket.com/mission-values/caring-communities/community-giving (accessed 14 November 2012).

Wilkinson, R. and Picket, K. (2009) *The Spirit Level: Why Equality Is Better for Everyone*, London: Penguin Books.

Wilson, E.O. (2002) *The Future of Life*, New York: Vintage Books.

Wintour, P. (2013) 'Fracking Gets Boost as George Osborne Bangs Drum for "Energy Revolution"'. *Guardian*, 5 August, available at: http://www.theguardian.com/environment/2013/aug/05/fracking-boost-george-osborne-energy (accessed 10 August 2013).

Young-Laing, B. (2011) 'Strategies to Prevent Displacement of Residents and Businesses in Pittsburgh's Hill District', presentation to Housing Justice Network National Meeting – Gentrifying Neighborhoods Workshop, Washington, DC, 17 October.

Index